THERE'S NO SUCH THING AS "THE ECONOMY"

Fig. 1. Hieronymus Bosch, *Ship of Fools* (1490–1500)

First published in 2018 by punctum books, Earth, Milky Way.
https://punctumbooks.com

ISBN-13: 978-1-947447-89-9 (print)
ISBN-13: 978-1-947447-90-5 (ePDF)

LCCN: 2018959825
Library of Congress Cataloging Data is available from the Library of Congress

Interior design: Annette Ding, Noah Feiwell, Stefani Villatoro, and Vincent W.J. van Gerven Oei
Cover design: Madison Mead

HIC SVNT MONSTRA

THERE'S NO SUCH THING AS "THE ECONOMY"_

Essays on Capitalist Value

Samuel A. Chambers_

to my teachers

Contents_

The Wells Fargo Story: Economics, Value and the Logic of Capital_

A Tale of Capitalism_

In September 2013, Scott Reckard, a veteran financial reporter for the *Los Angeles Times,* received a lead on a story from an editor, connecting him to an employee of the banking behemoth Wells Fargo. This employee, along with at least 30 others at the time, had been fired from local Los Angeles Wells Fargo branches for opening new accounts for existing customers — sometimes by manipulating the customers into agreeing to open the accounts and sometimes without even receiving customer permission to do so. On the surface, it did not look like much of a story, but the fired employee claimed that he and others were terminated simply for doing their job. He asserted that they were heavily pressured, and often coached, to do precisely what they had been doing — opening as many new accounts as possible for existing customers. And employees who failed to meet unreasonable goals for new accounts were directly punished: forced to stay late on evenings, required to work weekends, and denied routine perks. At the beginning of October 2013, Reckard published a short piece that reported the firings; it included statements from a Wells Fargo PR person, explaining that this "small number of team members" had, on their own, violated rules and ethical standards and been appropriately fired for their actions (Reckard 2013a). Reckard also described the one fired employee's account of undue pressure, but he did not mention the unverified claim that managers were explicitly coaching employees. It was a short, to-the-point, business-section story of only 400 words, and Reckard himself expected little to come of it.

Immediately upon its appearance, Reckard and the *Los Angeles Times* editorial offices were inundated by an unexpected response: "phones started ringing off the hook and the emails started landing from people all over the place. Mainly current and former Wells Fargo employees, but customers too. They wanted to tell stories about what had happened to them" (Vernon 2016). Thus began an intense, months-long period of investigative reporting, in which Reckard, along with other writers and numerous editors, interviewed dozens of Wells Fargo customers, employees, and former employees. They fact-checked and corroborated claims made by those interviewees with exhaustive research into the many legal suits brought against Wells Fargo in the recent past. The result, published on 21 December 2013, was a major piece of investigative journalism: an incisive indictment of a widespread culture of fraud and criminality at Wells Fargo, based upon powerful revelations of a systematic effort, running from customer service representatives all the way to the very top of the corporate structure, all designed to increase customer accounts at all costs. Cross-selling is the corporate name for this practice, and Wells Fargo was then, and remains at the time of my writing in late 2016, the "master" of cross-selling, averaging "6.15 financial products per household — nearly four times the industry average" (Reckard 2013b).

Reckard's big story remained focused on the employees themselves, describing the varieties of urgency they felt to meet wildly unreasonable goals, and laying out in specific detail the punishments handed down for those who failed to reach them. But unlike the first short piece, this story canvassed a wide swath of employees: lower level workers, mid-level managers, and more senior management. It included some who were fired, some who kept their job, and even some who went so far as to quit or retire because they could no longer endure the pressure and abuse. And Reckard's background research *connected* the accounts given by these employees, first to explicit sales targets set by Wells Fargo, and then to Wells Fargo's own consistent bragging in its earnings reports about its world-leading success at cross-selling. Linking the employees' experience with the earnings reports' celebration of the results was the *pièce de résistance*: concrete evidence of explicit training in methods of cross-selling, including coaching on how to inflate reported sales numbers.

For this larger story, Wells Fargo had their CFO Timothy Sloan agree to be interviewed by Reckard. Sloan stated baldly that he was "not aware of any overbearing sales culture" (Reckard 2013b). To back up claims like this one, two Wells Fargo PR spokespeople explained that the bank makes ethical conduct a priority and had even recently created an "Ethics Program Office." As evidence of the bank's rigorous commitment to these values, they pointed to the same recent firing of 30 employees (for cheating to reach sales goals) that had led Reckard to this story in the first place. To give one final, if indirect, refutation of the claim that these cheating workers were anything other than bad apples, Wells Fargo spelled out that bank tellers earn only about 3% in incentive pay anyway.

These claims proved hard to square with the bank's own internal documents and reports, as obtained by the *Los Angeles Times* during their investigation. Those documents showed how doggedly Wells Fargo focused on cross-selling goals, how closely they tracked these sales numbers, and how forcefully they pushed the growth of these numbers. Top executives referred to the ultimate goal as "the Great 8," meaning an average of eight financial products per household. The bank's PR language also proves hard to reconcile not only with the dozens of reports Reckard received from employees but also with the string of lawsuits brought against Wells Fargo by both customers and former employees. Customers repeatedly sued for having accounts opened in their names without their permission or even knowledge, actions that included the forging of customer signatures and the creation of fake businesses in customers' names. Employees sued for a plethora of reasons: for wrongful termination, given that they were fired for directly following orders (for example, in opening accounts in family members' names); for discrimination, given that many were unfairly punished for missing unreachable sales goals; and, in the case of managers, for unpaid overtime, given that they were forced to work extensive extra hours attempting to meet the sales goals missed by their staffers (Reckard 2013b).

The power of Reckard's investigative reporting centers on his neutral reporting of "both sides" of this story, but this is not because the two sides "balance." Rather, the force of the piece comes through by way of the deep tensions between them, and because in allowing Wells Fargo representatives the space to explain themselves, Reckard provides the time needed for their claims to ring *hollow*. The piece closes with a prescient flourish as Reckard returns to the story of one of the many customers in whose name new accounts had been opened without their knowledge or approval. This customer did not sue, but she did travel to her local branch to complain in person and request an apology. Instead of apologizing, the bank manager explained that the person who opened the account was one of the best employees at the branch. Reckard, maintaining his focus on the individuals involved, gives this customer the last line: "if that's one of your best employees, Wells Fargo is in trouble" (Reckard 2013b).

At the time, and for quite a while afterwards, that closing line might have looked like nothing more than the bitter complaint of the customer, or perhaps the writerly touch of the reporter. Reckard's "local" story did not become a major national issue, and over the next six months Wells Fargo stock maintained an uninterrupted upward march, rising from $44.96 on the day Reckard's story ran to $52.89 on June 20, 2014. But while Reckard's reporting made no dent in the 24-hour news cycle of the mainstream media, it turns out it was read closely by another party that matters.

Exactly three years to the month that Reckard first began researching the story, the US Federal Consumer Financial Protection Bureau (CFPB) fined Wells Fargo $100 million — the largest fine in the history of the CFPB. At the same time, they announced another $85 million more in fines to be paid to the Office of the Comptroller of the Currency, and to the City and County of Los Angeles. Pressured by lawsuits (and the discovery process attendant to them) and by the CFPB, Wells Fargo admitted — based on their own internal investigation — to the fraudulent creation of more than 1.5 million deposit accounts and more than half a million credit accounts, totaling more than $2.5 million in fees charged to customers (CFPB 2016). During this time, the bank also fired more than 5,300 workers for the very behavior that the CFPB declared was systematic, encouraged and intentional (Corkery 2016b).

Unlike Reckard's initial reporting from 2013, this time the story "blew up." *The New York Times* alone published 58 stories directly on or related to the Wells Fargo scandal in just over three weeks after the CFPB fine was announced. Wells Fargo CEO John Stumpf was immediately summoned to give testimony separately to both the Senate Banking Committee and the House Financial Services Committee. The effort to catalog the number of op-eds and blog entries calling for his resignation would require massive coordinated research, and "Wells Fargo" became a standard referent for corporate wrongdoing. But more important than the invective spewed toward the man at the top of the corporate structure is the broader reporting done on the scandal itself. Once the story broke at the national level, the incentive to report it more widely pushed journalists and bloggers to follow up on every angle. What they found was not pretty.

Even as Wells Fargo was firing thousands of workers for actions taken to meet patently unrealistic sales goals, the bank clung fiercely to exactly those same sales goals. Carrie Tolstedt, the Wells Fargo executive who maintained those goals and oversaw the group of "rogue" employees who had to be fired for their illegal and unethical actions, was rewarded handsomely for her management and leadership. Over the period under investigation by the CFPB, 2010–2015, Tolstedt received more than $20 million just in bonuses; her 2015 total compensation was more than $9 million. Serendipitously, during the CFPB investigation Tolstedt decided to step down from her position as head of retail operations, with plans to retire by the end of 2016. She left the bank with nothing but the highest of praise from the CEO, who said in July of 2016 that she was "a standard-bearer of our culture" and "a champion of our customers" (Gandel 2016). At the time, her departure compensation package was worth just shy of $125 million.

Follow-up reporting goes well beyond the numbers, however. During the CFPB investigation and in public statements since the fines were handed down, Wells Fargo admitted to knowing about sham accounts only since 2013, the time of Reckard's initial reporting. Yet there are now multiple class action lawsuits being pursued against the bank, by employees who claim they were fired not simply for failing to meet the sales goals, but specifically for reporting, both to managers and to Wells Fargo's own "ethics hotline," the opening of sham accounts by fellow employees. These lawsuits claim retaliatory action against the employees for their decision to follow exactly the ethical guidelines that Wells Fargo put in place. Moreover, many of these employees were fired long before 2013, and thus the suits themselves suggest that the bank had been informed of this behavior at least as early as 2010. Rather than investigate the behavior, the bank fired the employees who reported it (Cowley 2016).

What's Going On?_

I recount this tale in some detail, certainly because it illuminates a great deal about the status and ethos of neoliberal capitalism in the middle of the second decade of the twenty-first century. Yet I work through the narrative primarily so that I can pose a deceptively simple yet crucially important question: *what is this story about?* When Reckard ran his initial *LA Times* article on fired employees in October 2013, the story appeared to be mainly about the minor crimes of low-level employees, and surely Wells Fargo PR spokespeople today would still like to frame the narrative in those terms. At this point, however, no one — not even Wells Fargo executives, who, after all, did agree to the terms of the largest fine in CFPB history — is really buying such a framing of events. Whatever else we might say, it seems clear that this is not a tale concerning the malfeasance of low-level employees; this is not a story of petty crime.

Now that there is a palpable, concrete scandal in the air — made real by fines, lawsuits, and a media frenzy — we see and feel an overwhelming temptation to view this as an *ethical* story. The ethics frame perfectly captures the circus politics of CEO John Stumpf's appearance before various congressional committees, and it is surely various forms of morality that animate the self-righteous outrage — sometimes spewed, sometimes deftly articulated — by everyone from op-ed writers to average citizens, from TV pundits to US senators. No one can read the historical facts of this case without feeling viscerally that something is wrong here, and no doubt "wrong" resonates on an ethical level. The effect of this ethical frame is to insist that someone, somewhere, must have acted immorally or unethically, and this action must be the overriding cause and explanation of the complex series of events that unfolded. The ethical frame provides us a definitive "answer." If this is a story of ethics, then someone is to blame; our necessary response must therefore be to find that someone or multiple someones, determine their guilt, and above all else, *punish them for their actions.*

An apparent third way to view these events is to see them as a story about greed. Given that the narrative concerns a capitalist corporation, high finance, and huge sums of money, it fits nicely and neatly into this narrative structure, since there is a long history of interpreting the excesses of capitalism as the result of greed. However, I submit that greed and ethics are actually the same framing of the story; the difference is only a matter of scale or perspective. "Greed" provides what social scientists today call the "micro-foundations" for the ethical explanation of events.

In other words, "greed" is the answer to the question "why did they do it?" Once we see this as a story of ethics, we know that a wrong has been done and someone must be accountable. Greed enters the narrative at the point when our ethical frame has narrowed its focus to the responsibility of the guilty individual; at just this moment, greed provides us with the motive we seek to attach to the responsible party, for explaining the wrong that he or she has done. The 2016 Wells Fargo story therefore seems to be, fundamentally, an ethical story, a story of corruption, violation, and betrayal, motivated by narrow self-interest and greed.

It's Not About Ethics_

One of the primary aims of this book is to provide an alternative way of making sense of and responding to events such as those contained in the Wells Fargo story. I contend that this is not a story about cheating workers, unethical managers, or greedy boards of directors. The ethical frame proves utterly inadequate to capture what is going on here; worse still, the adoption of this frame blocks from our view much of what really is going on, and how and why it matters. I do not for a moment deny the existence of immoral or greedy actors as part of this tale, but I reject the idea of the overarching ethical frame as making sense of this story. The ethical frame seeks to trace the events back to individual causes. That is, the frame tells us that events transpired as they did *because of* individual actions, and that the cause of those actions was a failure by individuals to act ethically. This means that when we use the ethical frame to explain the story of Wells Fargo we necessarily presuppose a counterfactual story. In this hypothetical alternative no one cheats, no one is fired, no one is fined, and there is no scandal; all of the differences between this suppositional story and reality come down to the fact that in our counterfactual no one acts unethically, and no one is so blinded by greed as to break the law or violate the moral code.

Yet such a counterfactual proves to be utterly nonsensical — that is, not just unrealistic or impractical, but incoherent as a heuristic — because we can remove immorality from the narrative and still end up with the same exact results.[1] To see how, let us ask what happens if we throw off the ethical frame entirely: instead of assuming that the cause of events must lie with immoral actors, what if we assume that everyone in the story acted utterly reasonably and perfectly rationally? We can start with the low-level employees, bank tellers, sales clerks, and customer service representatives — precisely the individuals that make up the vast majority of the fired 5,300 employees. Everyone agrees that those individuals were given extreme, unrealistic goals for cross-selling; it was expected and demanded of these employees that they sign up existing Wells Fargo customers to more and more accounts, even though Wells Fargo already had a dramatically higher average number of accounts per customer than the rest of the banking industry. Indeed, even a court that sided with Wells Fargo in the lawsuit of a fired employee accepted as fact that these goals were impractical and unreachable (Cowley 2016). In addition to the sales goals themselves, which were tied to their compensation, employees faced daily pressure from managers to attain such goals, and lying on the other side of the positive encouragement were a set of explicit punishments; as I have noted, employees who failed to meet daily sales quotas were required to work late and on weekends. Moreover, there is widespread evidence that in many branches both other employees and managers provided advice, training, and coaching in setting up either legally grey accounts (those opened in family members' names) or outright illegal sham accounts. And finally, these very employees were able to observe what happened to other employees who either consistently failed to meet sales goals (they were fired) or who reported illegal practices to management (they were also fired).

---

1   Here I echo Mark Blyth, who takes a similar line in response to efforts to blame the 2008 financial crisis on immoral bankers. Blyth notes that the morality tale always tempts precisely because it comforts, yet it still fails to *explain*. Blyth puts it nicely, "you could have replaced all the actual bankers of 2007 with completely different individuals, and they would have behaved the same way during the meltdown: that's what incentives do" (Blyth 2013: 21; cf. Heinrich 2012: 16).

In the face of all of this, one rational choice would be to quit working for Wells Fargo and get another job. Many employees did just that (Reckard 2013b). But anyone working an entry-level job under post-2008 economic conditions faced a very soft labor market and therefore had no guarantees of alternative employment. Given all of this, wouldn't another viable, rational option possibly be to open (and then close) fake accounts in order to keep your job? Rather than describing the actions of these workers as immoral, we could see them as quite reasonable, if surely somewhat desperate. The fundamental logic is no different for mid-level managers. The only change is that this group often experienced even more intense harassment from their superiors, faced longer working hours (since many frequently had to compensate with extra work for the sales goals their employees missed), and confronted an even more hostile labor market (should they lose their job). Most importantly, the incentives for opening sham accounts were much greater for mid-level managers, who might see significant bonus salary for meeting sales targets.

One might respond to the above by saying that it misses the point: the ethical framing and explanation centers its focus not on the line-level employees but on the overall institutional structure, and particularly on the senior management. The buck stops at the top, and to understand what went *wrong*, to see where the immorality lies in the Wells Fargo story, we have to look up. And of course there is substantive merit to this response, since the congressional committees did not call in the fired Wells Fargo workers and accuse *them* of ethics violation; no, members of Congress directed their moral outrage and contempt in the direction of Wells Fargo's CEO, John Stumpf. During the weeks of September 2016, when the scandal unfolded along numerous axes, perhaps no single moment better captured the essence of the ethical framing of the story than the questioning of Stumpf by Senator Elizabeth Warren. Since the 2008 crisis, and even before being elected Senator, Warren has taken on the important role of Wall Street's fiercest critic, identifying herself as the average consumer's staunchest advocate. Warren's questions to Stumpf during his testimony before the Senate Banking Committee were perhaps the most "viral" elements of this scandal, replayed on network news, late-night comedy shows, and all across the internet:

> WARREN: Have you returned one nickel of the money that you earned while this scandal was going on? Have you fired any senior management, the people who actually oversaw this fraud?

> STUMPF: No.

> WARREN: Your definition of accountability is to push this on your low-level employees. This is gutless leadership. (Corkery 2016a)

When pressed by other senators to explain what was being done to return to the company compensation already paid out to the very executives who oversaw this fraud, Stumpf repeatedly claimed that the Wells Fargo board was in charge of that process, that he was not involved, and that he did not want to taint the investigation in any way. This line of demurral provided Warren perfect context for another zinger: "You keep saying, 'the board, the board'. You describe them like they are strangers you met in a dark alley. Mr. Stumpf, *you are the chairman of the board*" (Corkery 2016a, emphasis added).[2] These are satisfying lines to watch or to read. By focusing our outrage against the CEO, they solidify the ethical frame — first by giving a face to evil, and then by staging a representative confrontation with that evil. The same dynamic was in play whenever late-night comedy shows would call out Stumpf for his hypocrisy, a task easily accomplished simply by first narrating some of the basic facts of the scandal, and then running clips of recent Stumpf interviews where he talks about Wells Fargo's deep and abiding

---

2   Throughout this book, I will mark all added emphasis in quotations as such; unmarked emphasis in quotations is therefore present in the original.

commitment to ethical values, fair and good business practices, and so-called "corporate social responsibility." It is doubtless true: Stumpf's answers make him appear weak, cowardly, and immoral. The contrast between his bold rhetoric about values and his oversight of the systematic defrauding of his own customers makes him look like a hypocrite. Or better yet, and to speak the truth honestly and plainly, the entire *mise-en-scène* makes the Wells Fargo CEO out to be an utter asshole.

Yet if we can disentangle ourselves for a moment from the jouissance of watching a corporate CEO get his comeuppance from Elizabeth Warren and John Oliver, we might want to pause for a moment to ask whether we have answered the simple question I posed earlier — namely, what's *really* going on in the case of Wells Fargo? This pause is prudent because the ethical framing of the story has pushed us toward an answer that looks like this: well, John Stumpf, the CEO, along with Carrie Tolstedt, the head of retail, and perhaps a few other executives yet to be named...are assholes. That logic might well undergird satisfying moments of theater on late-night television, but it proves woefully inadequate as an overall interpretation of either the systematic defrauding of thousands of customers for millions of dollars, or the abuse and destruction of the careers (and lives) of thousands of employees.

As one attempt to make sense of this story I have asked readers to place themselves in the shoes of Wells Fargo employees. Given the natural sympathy readers might already have for fired low-level employees, this was perhaps an easy request with which to comply. Here's a harder one: what if we try to put ourselves in the shoes of John Stumpf? We should do so, I suggest, not because we want to sympathize with him, but because this exercise in constructed empathy could tell us a lot more about what's going on than the otherwise satisfying ritual of mockery and humiliation. Stumpf took over as CEO of Wells Fargo in June 2007 and hence began his tenure at the top of the corporate ladder by witnessing the crash of 2008, including the meltdown of Bear Stearns and the near collapse of numerous other financial leviathans. Between 2008 and 2012, 465 US banks failed. All of the US and parts of the global economy were in free fall, with most everyone in agreement — from academic experts to TV pundits — that we were entering either the next Great Depression, or at least the worst recession since the Depression. And last but not least, all of this was set off by disaster and scandal in the heart of the banking and finance industries.

It is in this context that we should consider a very basic question: what is the job of a CEO? The Wikipedia entry puts it nicely, describing a CEO as "charged with...*maximizing the value of the entity*" ("Chief Executive Officer," Wikipedia.com, emphasis added). The CEO must maximize value, and we know, in the modern publicly traded stock corporation, the "value of the entity" is almost always and everywhere understood with the phrase "shareholder value." Finally, I must point out the obvious — that "shareholder value" is nothing more than a euphemism for stock price. The job of the CEO is to increase, maintain, and maximize the stock price. So what did Wells Fargo's stock price (ticker symbol WFC) look like after Stumpf became CEO? In the middle of September 2008, a bit more than a year after Stumpf took over, and just as Lehman Brothers was filing for bankruptcy, WFC reached a high of $44.69, from which it would fall, over the course of the next six months, to a low of $8.01 on March 6, 2009. All of this background information helps to concentrate our question in terms of seeing things through Stumpf's eyes. As the CEO of a major international bank not only at a time of intense international crisis, but also at the nadir of trust in financial institutions, what do you do?

It would be almost impossible to attract new customers in the crisis environment, and the passage of the Dodd-Frank Act (2010) further limited the options for creating and selling new financial products.[3] Thus it makes perfect sense to focus instead on your current customers. But aside from the effects on cus-

---

3 The Dodd-Frank Wall Street Reform and Consumer Protection Act is by far the most significant law passed by Congress in response to the 2008 financial crisis and the most important piece of US Federal financial regulation since the reforms that followed the Great Depression. Among a host of other provisions, the law created the Consumer Financial Protection Bu-

tomer retention, quality customer service does not raise overall profits, and it surely does not increase profit margins (a magic metric for stock valuation). If you cannot add new customers or create wholly new products, then you need to maximize revenue from existing customers with existing financial products and accounts. How do you square that circle? By cross-selling, of course. Cross-selling offers the perfect solution to the problem of how to raise profits and margins in the financial industry post-2008. But it needs to be paired with a second overall strategy: an aggressive PR campaign designed to burnish your image as responsible and trustworthy — in this case, by distinguishing the Wells Fargo brand from the tattered image of a cutthroat and out-of-touch Wall Street. Such a campaign would associate Wells Fargo with the independent and down-to-earth values of the western United States, as distant as can be from "New York City." All of this sounds like a reasonable, plausible, and potentially effective approach to increasing value.

Unsurprisingly, the strategy I have just outlined in hypothetical terms is precisely the one that Stumpf pursued, and I cannot fail to add, it was wildly successful. From that low of just over $8 per share, WFC climbed steadily and climbed high, all the way to $58.34 in July 2015. That price increase was driven by two major factors. First, Wells Fargo enjoyed unparalleled and unprecedented success in increasing accounts per customer to a number greater than six — a level, as Reckard initially reported in 2013, more than four times the industry average (Reckard 2013b). Second, Wells Fargo basked in its reputation as "Wall Street's most squeaky-clean bank" (Lopez 2016), maintaining and maximizing its distance from the supposed corruption of Wall Street. To aid this image, Stumpf himself maintained a rigorous PR schedule, vigorously defending this ideal image of the bank. Indeed, even in the depths of the scandal in autumn 2016, Wells Fargo made no noticeable changes to its "Vision and Val-

---

reau; therefore, were it not for Dodd-Frank the story of Wells Fargo might not have been told it all.

ues" page on the website.[4] It is topped by a large, smiling photo of Stumpf, bordered to its right with a stylized pullout quote, in 24-point font, that reads: "Everything we do is built on trust. It doesn't happen with one transaction, in one day on the job or in one quarter. It's earned relationship by relationship" (Wells Fargo 2016). From there the text of the full statement opens with the most glaringly false claim imaginable: "documents such as this are rare these days in corporate America" — no, they are absolutely ubiquitous — and proceeds for a number of paragraphs through entirely predictable PR-speak.

It is easy to label all of this massive hypocrisy, as I myself have just done above, unable to resist pointing out that the very first, apparently meaningless, line of the text is itself a blatant lie. But it is *too easy*. To take this tack is to miss the bigger picture by getting trapped in the ethical frame (its pull is enormous). In other words, returning to the language I used earlier: calling Wells Fargo hypocritical is just another way of calling its CEO an asshole. None of this does a thing to help us understand what is at stake in the story or how we might fashion future alternatives. More to the point, in calling out Stumpf's hypocrisy, we fail to see the ways in which that apparent "hypocrisy" is actually called for by his job — how, in reality, it is nothing other than a rational result of his pursuit of the two-pronged strategy to increase shareholder value. Indeed, a corporate CEO today is *supposed to be a hypocrite*; it is an implicit (i.e., unwritten) part of their job description. The primary task of a CEO is to increase stock price, and this includes two elements: implementing unreachable sales goals to drive profits, and going on talk shows to pay tribute to the importance of trust, relationships, and com-

---

4 My account was originally written in September 2016 and refers to the Wells Fargo website as it existed at that time. Wells Fargo deleted Stumpf's photograph from the "Vision and Values" webpage after they removed him as CEO in October 2016, but the page itself, including the same text remained up for more than a year. Thanks to the Internet Archive's "Wayback Machine," the page as it was in September 2016 can still be retrieved, https://web.archive.org/web/20161114221820/https://www.wellsfargo.com/about/corporate/vision-and-values/index.

munities. To see this phenomenon illustrated more vividly, just watch a weekend US PGA Tour golf tournament: at some point during the long telecast, the network announcers will effectively pause their coverage of the golf to have an extended friendly chat with the corporate sponsor's CEO, who will never be there to talk about corporate profits — and certainly not to discuss golf — but rather to repeatedly underscore the corporation's abiding commitments to the community (and particularly some marginalized segment thereof). It is nothing but the height of intelligent rationality for every corporate CEO to both implement "initiatives" and "programs" centered on so-called Corporate Social Responsibility (CSR), while at the exact same time taking whatever cutthroat action is needed to drive up profits and margins in order to increase the stock price. Moreover, even this formulation slightly misconceptualizes the phenomena under discussion: *the CSR programs are themselves designed to drive up the stock price,* and thus from this perspective, there is no hypocrisy at all.

It's not that John Stumpf is *not* an asshole. Rather, in being an asshole he is doing exactly what a corporate CEO is supposed to be and do today.[5] The story of Wells Fargo, including the central

---

5   Relatedly, we might also say that it's not that Stumpf is not greedy, but that explaining capitalism by way of "greed" utterly misses the point. This reply holds for those who want to criticize capitalism as the outcome of actions of "greedy capitalists," and also for those who would attempt to vindicate capitalism through paeans to greed. As a powerful (even if fictional) example of the latter, we can take the famous "greed is good" speech, given by the character of Gordon Gekko, played brilliantly by Michael Douglas in Oliver Stone's *Wall Street* (1987). The speech is meant to argue for "greed" as the lifeblood of capitalist progress. But from the perspective I am developing here, we can say that, ultimately, this argument and others like it wind up missing the point, since the logic of capital renders "greed" redundant or superfluous. "Greed" designates a status of desire that is "inordinate"; to be "greedy" thus means to seek more than is reasonable or prudent. Yet this "more" — this extra, this super-abundant addition — already lies at the core of the logic of capital. To seek more — and then more, and more, and more — is the very essence of the primary logic of capital. If we equate this "more" with human greed, then we can only say that greed is essential to the normal functioning of the system. Perhaps this is Gekko's point, yet greed is

role played by Stumpf, should not be misinterpreted as a narrative about deviating from the straight and true path of ethical corporate behavior. Quite the contrary, this is just what corporate behavior looks like. In the end, we can say that just like the tellers who opened sham accounts, and just like the managers who coached them on how to do so, and later covered it up, Stumpf acted perfectly rationally.

Value Myths_

In insisting that the Wells Fargo story cannot be properly grasped through the ethical frame, I do not for a moment deny the importance of value both to this story and to the larger logic of capital. To the contrary, I want to stress that there is something intuitively right about what I have called the temptation of the ethical frame. What is going on here has something — in a way, *everything* — to do with values. However, the ethical framing of the story stands in the way of our seeing exactly how value and the logic of capital are bound up with one another. In this section, I will consider two potential replies to my efforts above to refuse the ethical frame (particularly to my efforts to make Stumpf out to be rational and prudent — to accept that he is an asshole, but to re-describe him as a *reasonable asshole*). These replies prove significant in their own right, but they play a particularly important role in the development of my analysis because, despite their stark differences, each centers on the question of value. Hence, in considering these arguments and in formulating a rejoinder to them, I will also begin to unfold my own, distinct account of the centrality of value to the logic of capital.

We can understand each of these hypothetical replies to my "empathetic" reading of Stumpf as efforts to give him more op-

---

therefore not a moral category at all. Greed is not good, but greed is also not bad. Greed is the very essence of the system, and it could only be questioned if we wished to question the system itself. This point anticipates my further elaboration on the idea of "the logic of capital," which appears in the final section of this chapter.

tions in terms of the decisions he makes as CEO. The first attempts to free Stumpf up directly, by arguing that his choices are not as limited as I have made them out to be — his chosen economic behavior can include a wider set of values than those of shareholders. I call this *the fiction of the myth of shareholder value*. The second response moves in just the opposite direction. It accepts most of my account of Stumpf's rationality, but argues that we can hem Stumpf in; we can limit his rational economic behavior with restrictions set by morality (in this way, we get Stumpf to choose differently by forcing him to do so). It seeks to constrain economic rationality by a set of value principles. I call this *the myth of a moral economy*. I will now briefly discuss both responses, in each case showing why they fail and analyzing how they construct the relation between economic actions or events (the logic of capital) and values.

There is now a small but certainly growing body of literature in both the financial press and in legal and business academic scholarship that calls my analysis of Stumpf into question on the most fundamental level. The central argument of these works can be stated succinctly as follows: the "law" of shareholder value is a myth and we must therefore broaden our understanding of viable and desirable corporate behavior. Perhaps contemporary economist Julie Nelson formulates the point most succinctly: "the 'maximize profits' idea is in our heads" (Nelson 2006: 50). In formulating my rejoinder, the finance magazine articles appear as low-hanging fruit. They all proclaim loudly, often in the very headline of their articles, that businesses and corporations can and therefore must do much more than maximize shareholder value (Blodget 2012; Denning 2015; Atwater 2016). Perhaps the clearest, and (for now) the most frequently cited, version of this argument comes from Marc Benioff, the multi-billionaire founder and CEO of Salesforce, who claims the following:

> The renowned economist Milton Friedman preached that the business of business is to engage in activities designed to increase profits. He was wrong. The business of busi-

ness isn't just about creating profits for shareholders — it's also about improving the state of the world and driving stakeholder value. (Benioff 2015)

There is neither subtlety in Benioff's rhetoric nor complexity in his logic. He simply wants to assert that corporations should be just as concerned with their employees and their customers (perhaps even with average citizens) as they are with their investors. This is what Benioff means by "stakeholders." While *stockholders* are literally the *owners of the stock* of the company, whose central and abiding concern is the value of that stock, *stakeholders* are anyone who has an interest in the outcomes or effects of the company's activities.[6] For Benioff, CEOs should concern themselves not with stockholders but with stakeholders, thereby making the world a better place. The business press reporters and columnists who cite Benioff will often add a list of reasons why exclusive emphasis on stock price (shareholder value) leads to negative consequences both for society as a whole and even, in the long term, for the firm itself (Denning 2014). Yet the central thrust of these business-press pieces is no different from the "values and vision" pages of major corporations: it ultimately serves to maintain and support the hypocrisy of the CEO as if it is not hypocrisy, by repeatedly insisting that CEOs can and should focus on all sorts of things besides shareholder value. But these same magazines and websites are simultaneously covering the rest of the financial industry precisely in terms of stock price, profit margins, and price-to-earnings ratios. Even within the individual articles that question the truth of shareholder value, the same authors admit that maximizing earnings

---

6   Benioff did not invent the stockholder/stakeholder distinction; it is now standard in contemporary corporate culture. However, it proves ironic, and a possible source of confusion, that in an effort to mitigate the singular focus on profit, the word "stakeholder" was chosen as the term of distinction. After all, both meanings of "stakeholder" in the *Oxford English Dictionary* refer either to "money" or to a "financial interest," and the word "stake" itself (on the basis of which the compound "stakeholder" is formed) refers directly to gambling.

per share leads directly to massive salary bonuses for the CEOs themselves (Denning 2014).

And while CEOs like Benioff can say whatever they want in *Huffington Post* blogs, the reality of doing their own jobs looks a bit different. This point was brought home in poignant and ironic fashion in early October 2016. Benioff, acting not as op-ed writer or philanthropist, but serving as CEO of Salesforce, had spent the preceding weeks talking up the possibility of his company acquiring Twitter. Given that almost everyone in the world knows Twitter, and almost no one outside of Silicon Valley or the business press knows Salesforce, these negotiations made headlines. But the headlines were not kind to Benioff. Here is a representative example from *The New York Times*, "Salesforce Shareholders Besiege Possible Twitter Deal" (Benner and Picker 2016). The story itself relates the intense displeasure of Salesforce's shareholders, particularly the mutual fund firm Fidelity Investments, who at the time owned approximately 14% of Salesforce's stock. Fidelity, along with a number of hedge funds and other investors, saw no stock growth "upside" to this acquisition, and they let Benioff know how they felt through phone calls, emails, and on- and off-the-record quotes to reporters. Benioff had been talking about the Twitter acquisition in the same grand tones and terms he used in his *Huffington Post* piece, and as early reports of the acquisition "talk" pointed out, from a stock price perspective it was not at all clear why Salesforce would be interested in Twitter, since the two firms operate on utterly different business models (Issac et al. 2016).

Perhaps Benioff thought that buying Twitter would help him to increase *stakeholder* value, or even make the world a better place. Alas, the sheer mention of acquisition talks, coupled with the bad press, sent the price of Salesforce stock down by 8%, and the movement of the stock price forced Benioff to act. In less than a week Benioff was scrambling to catch up: he called an investor meeting and set out to reassure not the stakeholders, but the *stockholders*. The main goal of the meeting was to convince investors that he heard them, and Benioff made it clear that because of the phone calls and emails from investors, "we have had to do a reset," which is business-speak for changing his mind. As Benner and Picker nicely articulate it, "The pushback offers a window into how big investors can exert pressure on would-be deals behind the scenes. Salesforce is particularly vulnerable to what its large institutional investors think because the unprofitable online software company relies heavily on its stock to make acquisitions and pay employee compensation. As a result, the company needs to keep investors happy for its share price to continue going up" (Benner and Picker 2016).[7] But if all of that were not clear enough about where Benioff, when acting as CEO, truly stands on shareholder value, this direct Benioff quote from the investor meeting says it all: "*we only do things that are in the interest of shareholders*" (Kim 2016, emphasis added). So much for improving the state of the world. But on the bright side, the result of these comments was a significant rise in Salesforce's stock price (Kim 2016).

Benioff's case illuminates the real force that "shareholder value" (i.e., investors demanding stock price gains) exerts upon a modern CEO. Some who have argued against the importance of shareholder value have done so based on a fundamental misunderstanding of that force. For example, the idea that maximizing shareholder value is nothing other than a myth, comes from the title of a book written by Cornell professor of law Lynn Stout, *The Shareholder Value Myth*. Stout's work serves as a complement and support both to financial press pieces designed to show that corporations, as people, can be good people, and to CEO paeans (like Benioff's) to making the world a better place.

---

7   This last line is a non sequitur since it holds true for any publicly traded company. If investors are "unhappy," meaning that they are selling rather than buying the stock, then its price will go down, regardless of the size of reported profits. For a perfect example of this phenomenon, just look at Apple stock movement from autumn 2015 to spring 2016. The stock plummeted, even though Apple reported not just large profits, *but the largest quarterly profits in all of corporate history* (Leswing 2016). There could be no better example of the basic truth that absolute profits do not matter; only profit growth matters, especially relative to the past. Moreover, stock valuations are almost always based on future projections, and if those are low, then the stock can drop today despite both profit and profit growth.

As her title boldly announces, Stout seeks to prove that shareholder value is a myth. But we need to be clear about what she means by that phrase.

Stout refers, both in her opening framing of the book and throughout the text, to the notion of "shareholder value thinking" and "the doctrine" of shareholder value (Stout 2012: 2). These terms connote a combination of both the general common wisdom and the explicit economic theory (which Stout, like Benioff, traces back to Milton Friedman) that shareholder value holds primacy in the decision making of the corporate firm. Importantly, Stout does not explicitly engage with economic theory or with the logic of the firm; her focus remains on the way that the common wisdom about shareholder value has morphed into a dominant ideology, particularly within law schools and business schools (Stout 2012: 114). Therefore, for Stout, the *myth* of shareholder value is the false belief that shareholder value is an actual *political law.* The best, most concrete work done in Stout's book centers on her debunking of the idea that US corporate law (at the federal or state level) actually *legally requires* CEOs to pursue shareholder value at all costs. In just this sense, we can say that Stout exposes and debunks the "myth" that there are legal requirements to increase shareholder value, or that corporate law contains a mandate to do so (the violation of which would allow shareholders to sue corporate CEOs) (Stout 2012: 3, 6, 25–31). In this sense, Stout's book proves quite effective at accomplishing the goals it sets for itself.

The problem with Stout's work, and the overall project to which it contributes, is that the myth she wants to debunk is itself nothing other than her own construction — a *fiction* she tells. Let me parse this key claim by starting with a primary assertion, labeled *p*. According to *p*, US law requires corporations to maximize shareholder value. A brief study of US corporate law, past and present, allows us to conclude that *p* is false; indeed, Stout's text nicely provides the evidence needed to reach such a conclusion. Yet here's the rub: Stout's book is not itself merely an argument for *not p*. Her argument presupposes as its very ground a distinct assertion, call it *q*. Q states that almost everyone believes the truth of *p*. The rhetorical force of *revealing* a claim or set of claims as *mythical* rests on the prior assumption that a large number of people (usually the vast majority) in a society also assert the truth of those claims, and may even hold those truths as primary elements of their belief system. However, aside from a few people so caught up in the corporate-speak of business schools and the financial press that they have internalized the truth of their own jargon, who actually believes that US law *forces* companies to maximize shareholder value? For the handful of people who really thought as much, Stout's book shows them why they were wrong about the basic facts.[8] Nonetheless, on the balance of the evidence, *q is false,* which is why I describe the general notion of "the myth of shareholder value" as itself a *fiction* — both presumed by Stout's starting point and propagated by her project.[9]

Moreover, on a broader rhetorical level, Stout's book actually contributes to the broad idea that the strength of the injunction "maximize shareholder value" should be considered on only legal or normative grounds (Stout 2012: 7, 32). Indeed, Stout herself can only understand the *force* of shareholder value as coming from outside the logic of the firm and capital; for her, it is imposed externally, either by legal requirements, or by philosophical arguments. Stout therefore believes that having undermined both of these bases for the injunction, the injunction itself simply ought to disappear. Corporations will then be free

---

8   To be fair to Stout, certain polemics against the corporate structure have carried the notion of a legal mandate out of business schools and into wider circulation. For example, in his attempt to lay all the evils of capitalism (if not of the world) at the feet of the corporate structure, Joel Bakan does indeed suggest that corporations are required by law to pursue profit, and in a case such as this, Stout's critique applies nicely (Bakan 2012: 225). This raises the opportunity for me to clarify that, in working through the Wells Fargo story, I have no intention or interest in repeating arguments like Bakan's. Bakan honestly believes that the problem is a bankrupt and soulless institutional form, while I am showing that such an institutional form itself arises out of the logic of capital.

9   Thanks to Sophia Hatzisavvidou for pushing me to think more deeply about the logic and rhetoric of myth.

to pursue a distinct and wider set of goals. This brings Stout's account right back around to align with Benioff's, with both upholding the following primary claim: *there is no such thing as the law of (shareholder) value.* CEOs and corporate boards are free to act as they wish.

I've shown how this logic worked out in the specific case of Benioff's company; now I wish to build on that account in order to consider the "law of value" in much more depth. Before making that move, however, let me quickly first consider the other response to my backhanded defense of Wells Fargo CEO John Stumpf. This one comes not from inside the business sector but from well outside it, particularly from academic discourses of moral philosophy. The central idea, as lucidly expressed by a recent representative example of this argument in *The New York Times* opinion pages, centers on taking on ostensibly "amoral" economy and making it moral (Davis 2016). Borrowing and analogizing from the well-established subfield in moral philosophy, "just war theory," Nathaniel Davis argues for a moral project that responds to economic logic. Despite rhetoric to that effect, the goal is not so much to make the economy itself moral as it is to *regulate* the economy according to the terms of moral philosophy. "Moral economy" thus describes not a new name for "the economy" or a reconfiguration of markets, but a new field in moral philosophy designed to check the excesses of the economic. As Davis puts it, "the principles of moral economy would seek to curb the market's more harmful excesses while preserving its societal benefit." These moral regulations and guidelines would produce what Davis calls "a 'just' economy," in which, for example,

> venture capitalists would consider the collateral damage (layoffs, defaulted retirements, etc.) that may result from their actions in the same way that military commanders must consider whether the use of a certain weapon in proximity to civilians would be discriminate and proportional. Chief executives would begin to care for their employees and their families the same way that professional

military commanders care for their troops and their families. (Davis 2016)

The rhetoric appeals; the vision entices. No doubt the above
paints an attractive alternative to today's grim realities.[10] Nonetheless, the *just economy* is a myth (much like the *just war* upon
which it is premised). Davis has done nothing to explain the
mechanism by which venture capitalists and CEOs would act
as he has them acting above, and without that mechanism his
descriptions amount to nothing more than wishes. In the following section I will say more about the myth of the moral
economy. But first I want compare the myth of moral economy
with the fictional tale of the myth of shareholder value, in order
to show how both contribute to the same overarching vision of
value in relation to economics.

Davis's discourse sounds both very similar to and quite distinct from that of Stout and Benioff. On the one hand, like them,
Davis envisions a world in which corporations and their CEOs
engage in a variety of practices and pursue a number of goals
that apparently have little to nothing to do with profits and stock
prices. On the other hand, unlike them, Davis suggests that in
order to make all of this possible, we need to develop a framework of moral rules that guide and regulate economic behavior.
Where Stout wants CEOs to know that the law does not *require*
them to maximize shareholder value, and Benioff wants to tell
CEOs they can choose to make the world a better place, Davis
claims that we need external rules that point CEOs in this moral
direction. The policy implications are therefore radically dis-

---

10 Under this broad heading, one might helpfully capture the entire project
of Corporate Social Responsibility (CSR), which includes a vast academic
literature on improved, ethical, and even utopian business practices. None
of this literature effectively grapples with the logic of capital, but CSR itself
can easily be understood to operate *according to the terms* of that logic — as
I have already shown in the case of Stumpf. Standard Operating Procedure
for corporate America today includes a heavy does of CSR language and
marketing, but none of it aims to alter or block the drive for profit; CSR
facilitates that drive. "Moral economy" and "corporate social responsibility"
are two sides of the same specious specie.

tinct. That is, one effect of a project like Stout's is to suggest that we do *not* need regulations to constrain corporate behavior, we only need to debunk the myth that law requires corporations to act in narrowly self-interested ways. In contrast, Davis is implying that policy makers will need to follow the lead of moral philosophers and implement specific rules and regulations that constrain corporations.

Despite such very meaningful differences, the philosophical discourse of moral economy and business discourse arguing against the primacy of shareholder value share a crucial underlying worldview: for both of them, *the realm of values lies outside of, utterly distinct from, the realm of "the economy."* In the case of Benioff and Stout, it is mostly a matter of the subjective values of the CEO or the board of directors; such agents must simply *choose* one set of values over another. In the case of Davis, values belong to their own sphere: the discourse of ethics and morality are part and parcel of the field of moral philosophy. Davis wants to construct the idea of a moral economy that controls economic behavior, but he never questions the conceit that economic behavior is just that — economic. Values come from elsewhere. Stout wishes to refute the notion that "maximize shareholder value" is a legal injunction, but for her the only other "injunctions" would be personal ones, based on the individual value choices a corporate entity makes. Both Davis and Stout leave fully intact the notion of an "economic sphere" as separate and separable from a values sphere.

The Law of Value_

These value myths *miss* something important that partially emerged in my narration of the Wells Fargo story, and which I now want to draw more fully to light. According to Benioff and Stout, there is no "law of value" because corporations are free to do whatever they want, including acting in the interests of stakeholders and the larger public. According to Davis, there could possibly be a "law of value," but it would be a *moral law* designed to restrain economic actors; it would be built from the materials of philosophy and then applied to the economic realm. Both approaches agree on two essential points concerning the rationality of actions taken within the sphere of the economy: those actions are A) amoral, and B) freely chosen. By "amoral," I mean that economic actions are not in and of themselves moral or immoral, since values lie outside the economic sphere, and by "freely chosen" I mean that economic choices are not dictated by rules or laws. Both points appear relatively uncontroversial, since it is standard treatment of economic behavior — both in the discipline of economics and in everyday discourse — to assume that economic actors are freely choosing actors, and that the economic sphere is not itself a value sphere.

This book argues that both assumptions are not just incorrect, but deeply wrong — wrong in ways that have major implications for both how we *grasp* the phenomena of political economy and how we *do* political economy, which in turn means not only how we study or understand the socio-politico-economic formation, but also how we shape and transform it. These false assumptions, built into the professional discourse of economics and woven into the common sense of capitalist societies, point to a fundamental misconception about how capitalism works — about what makes capitalism "capitalism." Moreover, this misunderstanding is not merely an academic one, since these misconceptions about the logic of capital actually feed into the very functioning and circulation of that logic. We can begin to unpick this knot of issues by refuting both assumptions as they operate within the myth of values.

First, the fiction of the myth of shareholder value is the effort to prove that there is no "law of shareholder value" — it is claimed to be a myth — by asserting the right of CEOs to make a different set of choices, leading to a different set of value results. *But the law of value is not a myth.* Yes, Stout is right to show that there are no legal requirements for CEOs to maximize shareholder value, but that does not mean there are no laws of value. A real set of forces operates on CEOs as they make their decisions. We saw this in detail in my reconstruction of Stumpf's actions, and it was brought home palpably when Benioff, the current and former champion of the idea that CEOs can and should choose to make the world a better place,[11] was instead forced to admit that, "we only do things that are in the interest of shareholders." Benioff's actions were so far from "free" that he had to drop the major plan that he had worked so hard on; he was constrained by a "law of value" that had nothing to do with legislation, regulation, or external ethical criteria.

Readers might balk at my use of the word "law" here. I would first note that I present the phrase in quotation marks, and I readily admit that the phenomenon I am describing operates quite differently from the principle by which H_2O changes from liquid to gas at 100°C. On the other hand, "law" is apt because it conveys both the sense of "capable of being demonstrated by reason" and the idea of a *force* operating on another body.[12] When Stumpf decides to make cross-selling the primary strategy of Wells Fargo's consumer banking divisions, and when Benioff decides to drop his Twitter acquisition strategy, both are acting in demonstrably reasonable ways, according to a set of discernible principles. They are also both operating under the constraint of a force; their actions are responses to that force

---

11 The idea of Silicon Valley CEOs claiming to "make the world a better place" has been much mocked — perhaps most famously by the HBO series *Silicon Valley*, which frequently targets this very trope. Yet when I refer to Benioff as a "champion" of this notion, I am not being sarcastic; I am merely describing his own position as laid out in the *Huffington Post* article I cited earlier (Benioff 2015). It would be easy to claim that Benioff is insincere — that he is merely posturing — but the critical force of my analysis has no need to resort to questioning the authenticity of Benioff's claims. I am quite happy to take him at his word, and then to show that even if he speaks sincerely, even if he is not in contradiction with himself, he remains in contradiction with the world.

12 These senses are conveyed in two of the *Oxford English Dictionary*'s entries on law, specifically those dealing with the phrase "law of nature": 9c accounts for law as "implanted by nature in the human mind," while 17 describes such law as indicating that "a particular phenomenon always occurs if certain conditions be present." This is this movement from a rational (and quite possibly divine) world, to a mechanistic (and quite possibly profane) one. My point in the text is not to invoke either full-blown sense of "law of nature," but rather to draw on the idea of a *force* that originates outside the self, acts on bodies, and cannot be dismissed as pure caprice.

(Heinrich 2012: 88). This is most clearly obvious in Benioff's case, since he is not doing what he wants to do, but doing what he thinks he has to do, subject to the constraints of shareholder value. We can see a real affinity, then, between the "law of value" and the "law of gravity," not because the former is a universal and 100% predictable law of nature, but because the latter can only really be understood as "force at a distance." The enduring mystery of gravity is that we can locate no direct, causal agent for it; outcomes occur subject to its laws, and it constrains our actions, but not in a way that can be fully specified locally. The law of value operates similarly in that its force is felt at a particular location, and it produces broad outcomes, but its direct source cannot be identified.[13]

Value and the Logic of Capital_

The mandate, the injunction, the *law* comes neither from statute nor from a substantive physical force, but from *the logic of capital*. I have had recourse to this phrase, "the logic of capital," a number of times in my discussion; I now want to clarify that usage and further elaborate this concept, which lies at the core of my project in this book. To begin, I need to underscore a few fundamental points. The logic of capital is neither an irresistible force, nor a predictable or deductive natural law. It operates only with and through human agency, meaning it is neither determinative nor determinist: it can be blocked, thwarted, undermined, or reworked. Further, the logic of capital is not the only logic that operates within a social order, as it works in conflict and in conjunction with a variety of other social, cultural, political, aesthetic, and ecological logics (see Glynos and Howarth 2007). This logic therefore operates *contingently*, functioning *only* within particular sorts of concrete social orders. This has two implications: first, the logic of capital is not transhistorical, in that it begins (and continues) to operate if and only if certainly prior historical conditions are brought into being; second,

---

13 The same is true of the "law" of supply and demand.

what will result from the functioning of that logic can never be known in advance nor understood outside of that concrete context in which it operates.

For all of these reasons, the logic of capital is neither the preeminent nor the ultimate logic, and I use the idea of this logic, as it operates within a specific social order, as a radical alternative to other accounts that would treat "capitalism" as a determinist and irresistible system. Nevertheless, when I insist that the logic of capital is not singular, complete, or all-encompassing, I do not deny, but rather clarify, the importance and power of that logic as a force within society. As I will discuss in more detail both below and in the coming chapters, the logic of capital helps to organize the social production and reproduction of society. This logic not only circulates goods and services through market exchange, but also structures and governs the way in which a social order produces, and it thereby plays a central role in the distribution of material wealth and well-being.

And this brings me to one of the central claims of this book: *the logic of capital can only be understood in relation to and in terms of value.* To demonstrate and flesh out this indispensable point it helps to go back to the pre-history of modern economics as a rich site for reconsidering the question of value. From the seventeenth through the nineteenth centuries the emergence of merchant and later industrial capitalism as genuinely new economic forms gave rise to political economy as the study of those forms. At the very heart of this new area of inquiry was the question of *value*. Under the earlier, feudal system, value was understood to emanate from the land itself.[14] There was thus

---

14 This claim oversimplifies for the sake of telling the story succinctly. It might be better to say that the idea of value emanating from land only really appears as *one* answer to the value question, and it does so largely *after* feudalism begins to break down. For mercantilist theory, value comes more from national production or balance of trade surpluses than it does directly from land; this notion still presupposes that land serves as a source for value, but the assumption remains tacit until the emergence of merchant capitalism starts to call it into question (since merchant capital seems to generate value independently of land as a source for value). In addition, a number of classical economists suggest that value comes from gold itself (an idea ridiculed

a strong symmetry between "political" and "economic" structures, so much so that these "domains" were inseparable: the social order was made up of lords with title to the land and serfs bonded to work the land for them. Value came from the land and the broader table of values was sharply reflected in the hierarchy of the social order. *Economic value and ethical-political value were therefore isomorphic.*

By the time that Adam Smith published *The Wealth of Nations* in 1776, this feudal system — though still in practice in many parts of Europe, and still present broadly in laws, norms, and customs — had been breaking apart for at least two centuries. The transformation of feudalism was wrought by the appearance of an entirely new merchant class (the bourgeoisie), whose wealth and power came not from the land or their titles to it, but from their own activity in trade and industry. The bourgeois revolution not only wreaked havoc on the structures and institutions of feudal society, but also split apart the politico-economic unity of value under feudalism. This was because the bourgeoisie — with no basis in land — itself seemed to bring about *new value* in the form of unprecedented new wealth and the attendant establishment of political power.

Hence, for the century prior to the appearance of Smith's famous book, less-famous writers had already been vigorously debating the question of value, and proposing explanations for the emergence and structure of value within the newly forming social order. William Petty (1662), Richard Cantillon (1755), and James Steuart (1767) had all developed alternative accounts of value that could make sense of and fit within the terms of a rapidly growing merchant society; each made some variation on the case that *both land and labor* were sources of value. At

---

by the more famous classical political economists, especially Marx). Overall, we can say that classical political economy deals with the problem of value thrown up by the fact that, as feudalism breaks down, value appears to be generated from a variety of sources: the mining of minerals, production processes under a division of labor, agricultural labor tied to corn or wheat (*blé*), and generalized systems of commodity exchange (Rubin 1979 [1929]; Dobb 1973; Mirowski 1988; Mirowski 1989).

the same time, the Physiocrats in France, particularly François Quesnay (1924 [1759]),[15] were attempting to understand the growth of capital — a unique phenomenon, with no direct parallel in the feudal order — as the production of a *surplus value*.

We can only grasp the meaning of the central texts of classical political economy in the context of these foundational, organizing debates over value. Smith sought to describe the new social order that was emerging, but he also wanted to further its development. Both tasks required him to advance a theory of value, and by drawing from the work of the previous century, Smith did just that. David Ricardo, in turn, can be understood to make one of his most profound contributions to political economy in the way that he criticizes and reformulates Smith's theory of value. Karl Marx, finally, develops what he consistently calls "a *critique* of political economy" — a critique of the entire field, not just particular contributions to it — by fully transforming and reworking the concepts of *value* and *surplus value*.

This thumbnail sketch is not meant to substitute for a history of economic thought in this time period, nor to stand in for a rigorous analysis of the general and specific theories of classical political economy. But it does raise at least two paramount questions: why did the question of value disappear from the study of political economy after the nineteenth century, and more saliently, what is the significance of this disappearance for our capacity to understand "politics" and "economics" today?

I place the terms *politics* and *economics* in quotation marks to highlight and place in question the idea that, in contrast to nineteenth-century political economy, these are understood today to be distinct academic disciplines, each corresponding to its own separate empirical domain. More radically, I take the following as a point of departure for, and as an explanatory goal of, this book: *there is no such thing as "the economy."* Our only

---

15 Mine is not a strictly historical project, but it does depend upon historical context. It would be cumbersome to provide the original publication dates each time I cite a source, so I will instead only provide original publication dates in brackets in those contexts when it proves particularly helpful and clarifying — and I will only do so the first time I cite that particular source.

field of inquiry is an overlapping, uneven, discontinuous, and non-bounded domain, made up of intersecting threads that are political, cultural, social, economic, and much more still (Chambers 2014). This is not to do away with "economics," since we can discern an economic logic within a social formation, and we can trace the effects of that logic historically. But to do either, we must first conceptualize that logic *as itself made possible by prior historical conditions* (which are much more than simply economic) and as always interacting with a broader socio-natural and techno-political assemblage.

It is only because the discipline of modern economics hypostatizes and continually reifies a domain called "the economy" that we (think we) can eliminate the question of value from the broader inquiry into the economic. We can see this decisively by picking up, almost at random, just about any contemporary economics textbook. Take Paul Samuelson's *Economics* — first published in 1948, it remains a standard text today. Its own authors describe the teachings of this textbook as thoroughly "centrist" in its positions on economic debates, and like every other introductory textbook, *Economics* takes care to distinguish rigorously between the scientific study of economics and less objective approaches.[16]

> When considering economic issues, we must carefully distinguish questions of fact from questions of fairness. Positive economics describes the facts of an economy, while normative economics involves *value* judgments. (Samuelson and Nordhaus, 2010: 6, emphasis added)

The authors go on to explain that so-called "normative economics" is not really economics at all: although genuine "economic analysis can *inform*" debates over value, those debates them-

---

16 Mirowski comments impolitely but accurately: "Samuelson very much encouraged the now prevalent attitude that economics is what economists do, as long as it looks scientific" (Mirowski 1993: 343)

selves belong properly in other, non-scientific, fields.[17] In their ubiquity, statements like these appear banal, but I quote them to underscore a crucial point: modern economics, by definition, explicitly excludes the study of value, yet that same field traces its roots to classical political economy.

Given the centrality of value to the historical foundations of modern economics within the field of nineteenth-century political economy, *how is this exclusion of value possible?* That question could be understood historically, as in: how did economics develop such that it could come to exclude that which had initially lain at its core? It can also be understood conceptually or theoretically, as in: is this exclusion of value tenable? This is not a book in the history of ideas; hence I do not take up the historical question directly, even though it surely relates to the work I do here. For my purposes, the shortest version of the story will do: after the so-called "marginalist revolution" of the 1870s (putatively carried out "simultaneously" by William Stanley Jevons, Léon Walras, and Carl Menger[18]), the neoclassical model becomes hegemonic, serving as the core of the discipline of economics throughout the twentieth century. And one of the most

17 My project here rests and builds upon an older set of debates between positivists and their critics. As I read that material, it seems clear that the latter won decisively: there is no such thing as a "value-free" realm, and no such thing as a fact that is not *value-laden*. Every elemental "fact" itself has a normative orientation or "spin" (to borrow a metaphor from quantum mechanics) (Taylor 1985; Connolly 1987). Therefore, when I challenge "ethical critiques" of capitalism, it is not because I seek a "purely scientific" account; rather, "positive economics" and "moral economy" are bogus for the same reason — each presupposes separate realms for "values" and "facts." This means that the sort of critical account of the logic of capital that I detail here can surely be called *ethical* in many important senses; however, ethics does not serve as a separate ground of critique of economics precisely because "the economic" and "the ethical" are bound up with one another. This conclusion has numerous implications, but one significant one worth mentioning here is that it changes entirely the nature of what we would call "exploitation" (see Arthur 2004: 46–57; cf. Cohen 1979).

18 This is the standard narrative; for a compelling argument that Menger was only included as one of the "discoverers" well after the fact, and perhaps for dubious reasons, see Mirowski 1988: 22.

profound effects of the work of marginalists and neoclassicals was to fully displace the value debates that anchored classical political economy (Mirowski 1989). As Jevons famously put it, "value depends entirely on utility" (Jevons 1971: 2). Hence the concept of marginal utility eclipses any need to study value; instead, a full-blown theory of price and equilibrium (coupled with some variant of marginal productivity theory) will suffice.[19] Setting this fascinating and important history aside, I focus on the theoretical question.

In doing so, I start with a working hypothesis that this book itself serves to demonstrate as one of its central theses: *economic forces establish, transform, and maintain relations of value.* In other words, it proves impossible to separate economics from questions of value (as the textbooks all purport to do) because value relations come to be in the world by way of economic logics. This means that "positive economics" is nothing more than a contradiction in terms. Samuelson and Nordhaus expel "value judgements" from the project of economics, but what is price if not a "judgement" — made by the market, but a judgement nonetheless — of *value*? Despite their claims to the contrary, neoclassical price theory cannot help but be a (disavowed) theory of value — though not a very good one (see Mirowski 1989). At the same time, it proves essential to highlight the other implication of my argument that economic forces produce relations of value: it rules out any *ethical critique* of economics, in the sense that one would somehow call economics into question from a

---

19 This displacement of value theory by marginalism is itself largely eclipsed/ forgotten by modern economics' dismissal of the history of economics. However, one can find many moments within that history, especially in the first decades after the "revolution," when economists proved themselves quite lucid about what was at stake in the "discovery" of marginal utility. J. B. Clarke offers one helpful example: "marginal theories...undermine the basis of Marxian surplus value doctrine by basing value on utility instead of on labor cost and [they] furnish a substitute for all forms of exploitation doctrine, Marxian or other, in the theory that all factors of production... receive rewards based on their assignable contribution to the joint product" (Clarke 1946 [1931]: 64–65; quoted in Dobb 1973: 166).

location that lies outside of it. If the logic of capital produces value relations, then moral philosophy has no monopoly on ethics.

At this moment, some readers may wish to protest: am I not "equivocating" when I use the same word, "value," to refer to two utterly distinct phenomena — namely, the economic commensuration of commodities, or valuation of goods in terms of price, on the one hand, and *moral values,* on the other? And if we make the proper separation of these two elements, then would it not in fact be correct to say that economics is the study of value in the sense of the price of commodities and the utility of objects, while moral philosophy is the study of moral and ethical value (of value systems and value judgements)? In response, let me start by saying that "to equivocate" means "to use ambiguous language so as to conceal the truth or avoid committing oneself" ("equivocate," New Oxford American). When I use the one term, "value," I am not being ambiguous about which *type* of value I mean. Just the opposite — I am using but one term so as to indicate clearly, to commit myself fully, to the idea that value does not come in distinct varieties or types (cf. Huber 2017). My project in this book refuses in its premises and refutes in its conclusions the very idea that there are distinguishable domains of value, or that "economic value" can be typologically separated from "moral value." Therefore, when I claim that economic relations and logics serve to produce and maintain relations of value, I do not say "economic value" (or price or utility) because I do not mean "economic" value; I mean value, period. The value relations that economic logics establish cannot be separated or excluded from morality and ethics. Indeed, it might be worth asking where this idea — of the natural separation of moral and economic value — comes from in the first place.

The *Oxford English Dictionary* provides 31 distinct entries for the noun "value." The bulk of those entries all relate directly to the idea of value as I have been using it here, and as it was taken up as a subject of investigation by classical political economy — namely, "worth or equality as measured by a standard of equivalence," along with a variety of associated meanings connected to exchange, quantity, amount of a commodity, the worth or usefulness of a thing, and so on. In all of these entries, and even across distinct meanings, "value" does not bifurcate between "moral" and "economic" domains. Indeed, only *one* of those 31 entries could arguably be read to suggest a distinct idea of moral values: "the principles or moral standards held by a person or social group; the generally accepted or personally held judgement of what is valuable and important in life" ("Value," OED). But even this meaning (originating quite late — the mid-nineteenth century — and first appearing in the United States) suggests the idea that individuals and groups have or express *personal* values, much more than it denotes a separate sphere of moral values. To get at the notion of moral values as used by the moral philosopher, we have to turn from the list of entries that are definitions to the list of compounds. Here we find "value judgement," "value-neutral," "value pluralism," and "value system" — all of which connote the type of separate domain of morality that one might call upon as distinct from economic value. Significantly, however, all of these compound entries are quite recent. Whereas the main entries for value typically date back to the fourteenth through sixteenth centuries, all of the compound entries with "moral" connotations date to the late nineteenth to mid-twentieth centuries. In other words, value as a "moral" term only emerges *after* the marginalist revolution in economic thought; this new and distinct idea of value only appears after the neoclassical paradigm has itself displaced and suppressed the older idea of value that centers classical political economy. This raises the possibility — one I cannot explore here — that we might owe the very idea of the separation of economic from moral value to the peculiar historical development of economics, along with the rise of other "social sciences." In any case, this discussion serves to show that the burden of proof should fall on those who seek to separate "moral" and "economic" value. In other words, the neoclassical economist must prove that price and utility have nothing to do with so-called moral values; the moral philosopher must demonstrate that ethics is separable from economics.

None of this is to deny the existence or importance of ethics or moral philosophy; it is rather to claim that the *work* economic logics do, and the *work* that moral philosophers do, both play out on the same terrain — that of society itself, the very social order which comes to champion or affirm some values and to denigrate or dismiss others. From the assertion, "there is no such thing as the economy," we can immediately derive a crucial corollary: "there is no such thing as the moral *sphere* or the ethical *domain*." Just as the logic of economics operates across the so-called domains of the cultural, the political, the social, etc., so too does the logic of ethics or the project of moral philosophy function across those same areas.

Given all of this, perhaps my earlier formulation is not thoroughgoing enough, since the idea that "economics *establishes* relations of value" could still be interpreted in such a way as to suggest that value itself somehow still remains external to economics. In other words, one might admit that economics *affects* value, but still want to plead that economics itself is surely something *other* than value. This book will consistently (perhaps mercilessly) reject such a plea. Indeed, as Philip Mirowski has brilliantly shown, trying to claim (within late nineteenth-century political economy) that value was separate from or external to economics, would be just like trying to claim (within mid-nineteenth-century physics) that *energy* was separate from or external to physics. Rather, just as energy became the unifying matter/process of physics during this time period, so did value become the unifying matter/process of the neoclassical paradigm of economics.[20] Mirowski demonstrates this point

---

20 Mirowski sums up the position in the form of a forceful critique of the entire history of neoclassical economics, which he describes as a program that has "misled generations of students by suggesting that it has relinquished all attachment to theories of value, when in fact the theory of value patterned on a conservative vector field is the only thing that holds the program together" (Mirowski 1989: 399). I thus see Mirowski's historical work as a powerful complement to my efforts here, since he helps to explain the disappearance of value from modern economics, not as a natural progression (toward empirical truth), but as an active suppression. Mirowski shows that neoclassical economics never really stopped being about value, even

through in-depth readings of all the major thinkers from political economy, yet I can illustrate the main contours of the point through a brief synopsis of Marx's "definition" of capital.

Put simply, Marx defines capital itself in terms of value. For Marx, capital is not a concrete object that can be pointed to or measured empirically. Capital is a particular social relation, which means that "capital" only exists — that is, comes to be — within a social order that produces and reproduces that definite social relation. Marx refuses the reduction, so common today, of the logic of capital to the idea of market exchange. As Marx explains, markets for the exchange of equivalent commodities existed long before the historical emergence of capitalism, and even within the terms of a roughly "capitalist system" it is quite possible to see the function of markets as separate from the logic of capital. That is, when I come to market with a commodity (C) and exchange it for another commodity (C), I exchange equivalent for equivalent ($C \to C$), and in this exchange we see no sign of capital. Even when I use the intermediary of money, first selling my commodity for money ($C \to M$), and then using the money to buy the second commodity ($M \to C$), I still complete a process of equivalent exchange; the money only mediates the transfer, and capital still never appears. Marx shows, however, that the simple fact that market commodity exchange can be broken down into two temporally distinct acts makes it possible for markets to be used for purposes *other than* the exchange of equivalent commodities. Hence, if I come to market with money (M) and exchange it for a commodity ($M \to C$), only then to later sell that commodity for more money (M'), I have helped to foster the circulation of capital (and not the mere exchange of equivalents). In this latter case, the overall movement is $M \to C \to M$. Yet the second M cannot be the same as the first (hence the nomenclature of M') since the entire point of the operation is to use money to get *more money*. Furthermore, just

---

though it had to do more and more work to pretend as though it were not about value at all — precisely because its understanding of value was compromised from the outset.

as money was largely beside the point in the original exchange of equivalents, so commodities are apparently beside the point in the circulation of capital. Thus, the equation of $M \rightarrow C \rightarrow M'$ *reduces,* as it were, to $M \rightarrow M'$.

Capital is the logic by which money begets more money. At the same time, money is nothing other than the form that value takes under a system in which the logic of capital preponderates. Marx summarizes as follows:

> In simple circulation, the value of commodities attained at the most a form independent of their use-values, i.e. the form of money. But now, in the circulation M–C–M, value suddenly presents itself as a self-moving substance which passes through a process of its own, and for which commodities and money are both mere forms. (Marx 1990: 256)

Value, Marx says, becomes the very "subject" of the overall process, in the sense that the logic of capital is itself a movement and growth of *value* — a movement that arranges other elements around it by prompting the movements of material and the actions of individuals. This is the sense in which Marx declares that the "valorization" (*Verwertung*) of value under the logic of capital is a self-valorization (*Selbstverwertung*). Rearranging terms, we can say that capitalism is the self-valorization of value (Marx 1990: 255).

To study the economics of capital is to try to understand value, which in turn means to grasp value's *movement* — its expansion and contraction. At its core, this is what I mean by "the logic of capital." In what follows, whenever I describe or call upon "the logic of capital," I mean to draw to the reader's mind this strange and significant process by which value valorizes itself — value produces more value; money begets more money; M becomes M'. As I have shown, the *logic of capital* as the self-valorization of value is related to but should not be conflated with the idea of a *system* of capitalism. Therefore, in calling on this logic, I eschew the idea of dichotomizing "capitalist systems" and "non-capitalist economic systems."[21] Rather, my aim is to call attention to the specific shape, impact, and results that the logic of capital may have within a particular social formation.

Thus, to return to our CEOs — Stumpf, Benioff, and others — we can say the following: given the logic of capital, a CEO *does* have to increase shareholder value, since the CEO's task is to oversee, maintain, and support the valorization of value. The CEO *must* increase (shareholder) value, not because failing to do so is illegal or unethical, but because such a failure thwarts the logic of capital itself. Value (profit) used to support workers and communities is, when thought within the terms of the logic of capital, wasted value, since it is value that can no longer self-valorize. This is why Marx is always at pains to compare and contrast the proper efforts of the capitalist with both hoarding, on the one hand, and luxurious consumption, on the other. Consumption destroys value, because commodities consumed are no longer values at all (Marx 1990: 228). Hoarding preserves value as value (hence the close similarities between hoarders and capitalists), but fails to augment that value. The capitalist must neither consume M' nor hold on to it. He must throw it back into the circuit of capitalist circulation, returning M' to its original status as M, so that it can become a new M'. This is why Marx calls the capitalist a "rational miser," because he preserves M in order to transform it into M' (Marx 1990: 254).[22]

And this is also why a "high" stock price is meaningless. It does not matter that Google (GOOG) is trading at $800 and Ap-

---

21 This point helps to explain why I place to one side the "varieties of capitalism" literature, since my goal is not to typologize different "systems" but to follow the logic of capital in different contexts. From this perspective, a table of capitalist types make very little sense, since every expression of the logic of capital within a concrete social order will be unique. Moreover, in later chapters I call on an understanding of historical development that proves incompatible with typologization: if new historical forms are truly new, then no typology can capture them. Thanks to Sebastián Mazzuca for prompting me to clarify this point.

22 Marx also wishes to suggest that a certain miserliness lies at the core of the logic of capital, and so he calls the miser "a capitalist gone mad" (Marx 1990: 254).

ple (AAPL) is trading at $100. What matters is how much each has *gone up* in the past day, the past quarter, the past year, and so on. The CEO who used profits to "change the world" would act like the consumer, destroying value for other ends. And the CEO who wanted merely to maintain profits or stock price would act like the hoarder or miser, preserving value but failing to increase it. This logic sheds light on a change in language that post-dates Marx by more than a century, but which he might have appreciated: the use of "grow" as a transitive verb, applying to something other than farm crops or human hair.[23] The CEO must "grow the business" precisely so as to facilitate the valorization of value.

To do otherwise, as we already know, will by definition disappoint "Wall Street," and with it the board of directors — thereby ultimately leading to the CEO either making less money (at best) or being fired (at worst). To return to Stout's thesis for a moment, we can reply to it quite plainly: saying that a CEO does not *have to* increase shareholder value is like saying that someone who works at a car dealership does not *have to* maximize the number of cars he or she sells every month. Certainly, salespeople could spend more time getting to know each customer or helping with after-sales clients who need service or support. They *could do* all sorts of things, but if they want to earn more money, or perhaps just keep their job, they have to sell more

23 The change in linguistic usage can serve as a mirror, after a temporal delay, for the debate between the Physiocrats, on the one hand, and classical economists like Smith and Ricardo, on the other. The Physiocrats argued that only agricultural labor was productive labor, because only agriculture produced a surplus — in the very literal sense that the autumn harvest reaped a surplus that was not physically present at the spring planting. Smith and Ricardo, in their respective turns, replied by asserting that abstract labor was itself productive. In effect, they were saying it was possible to actively "grow value" with industrial labor in the way we grow wheat and corn with agricultural labor. This dispute explains Smith's intense fixation on "division of labor" and his eagerness to make the division of labor (rather than technology or anything else) the causal source for labor productivity. By attributing productivity to division of labor, Smith inverts the Physiocrats' argument that only agricultural labor is productive while industrial labor is sterile (Quesnay 1924; Smith 1999 [1776]; Ricardo 2001 [1821]).

cars. It feels odd to even need to spell this out, but in the face of all the protestations about how maximizing shareholder value is unnecessary, it seems worthwhile to emphasize and specify exactly how it is essential, if not compulsory.

If Benioff and Stout are wrong to assume that CEOs can act completely freely, that they are not subject to the law of value, then Davis is wrong to think that moral economy could regulate economics by imposing standards of value on it from outside. To dispel the myth of moral economy,[24] I need to return to, and develop more fully, an idea I mentioned earlier and which functions as the most important general point of this book. I will start with the following version, formulated in direct response to the project of moral economy: we cannot regulate the economy by way of an exterior system of values, because as I have shown, one of the primary things that the logic of capital does is to *establish relations of value.* "The economy" is not a value-free or value-neutral sphere, because economic relations themselves prove to be value relations. ✁

Notice that this claim is not the more anodyne assertion that there are moral *implications* of economics. Economists would call these externalities: side-effects or consequences of economic behavior that are not themselves accounted for within economic rationality. Textbooks usually offer the manufacturing plant that pollutes the water or air as their prime example; hence, if society values clean air and water, then it will need to regulate the plant to limit its external (non-economic) impact. As the very name of the concept so clearly shows, "externalities" reinforce the idea that the economic sphere and the value sphere remain utterly separate.

My contention proves distinct from these more common notions. In arguing that economic relations and logics themselves *establish relations of value,* I am first of all calling into question the very idea of "the economy" as a separate, amoral domain.

---

24 Here I hold onto the language of "myth" exactly because Davis's narrative advances a "widely held belief," one that I am trying to show "is false" — i.e., the very definition of "myth" ("myth," New Oxford American Dictionary).

An "economic" event is never just economic, and it never happens only in or to "the economy." As I suggested above, *the* so-called "economy," understood as a discrete object or domain, only comes into existence as a construction of the discipline of economics, after which the very idea of such a place or thing is reified by other disciplines (who explicitly or tacitly accept the idea that "the economy" is what economics studies). Every social order is woven together by threads that are simultaneously economic, political, cultural, and so on (Chambers 2014). Just as the economic, the political, and the social do not exist in, nor can they be confined to, separate spheres, so too for "values." There is no moral domain, separable from others.[25] Values and value systems are themselves built into, developed through, and secreted out of larger social orders. If we want to understand value relations we cannot look to a discrete object or a separate value sphere; we can only ever look at society. This line of argument entails the very impossibility of placing "the economy" on an ethical foundation, for the straightforward reason that one of the things "the economy" does is produce and restructure value relations.

The form that value takes in a society structured according to the principle of capital is itself dependent upon the logic of capital. That logic, which regulates the circulation of capital, also gives rise to values. Therefore, we cannot ground the economic in ethics any more than we can simply regulate it with a so-called "moral economy" (which, as I have already shown, is not really a type of "economy" but a type of moral philosophy). What we mistakenly call "the economy" is better understood as a logic that operates "across" many putatively discrete domains (e.g., the social, the cultural, the political). And through the operation of this logic, "the economy" is therefore also a "place" where value relations are produced and sustained. Value can-

---

25 Marx makes an apropos and incisive comment when he says, "to clamour for equal or even equitable retribution on the basis of the wages system is the same as to clamour for freedom on the basis of the slavery system. What you think just or equitable is out of the question" (Marx 1995: 18; see also Mann 2010: 175; Huber 2017: 41).

not be excluded from "the economy" because the logic of capital is a value-producing, value-supporting, and certainly a value-transforming logic.

Through its very own logic and operation, a capitalist economy actively constructs what we would only later misrecognize as its so-called normative foundations. From this perspective, we can restate the problem with the ethical frame that is so frequently applied to economic stories in the twenty-first century, and which I have been trying to break apart from the beginning of this chapter. The ethical frame reifies the false assumption that the economic and the moral are separate realms, thereby making it impossible to see the way in which they are mutually intertwined. This means that, in viewing events through the ethical frame, we fail to see the logic of capital itself at work, because the logic of capital is indissociable from the law of value. Indeed, we can reformulate this paramount point to say that *the logic of capital is a law of value.* If we cannot understand the manner and extent to which the logic of capital establishes relations of value then we fail to grasp, and/or we fundamentally misrecognize, that logic itself. Without an understanding of the law of value, of value relations, *of the value-form,* we cannot understand capital(ism) at all. This book aims to establish just that understanding — to grasp the logic of capital *as* a law of value.

CHAPTER TWO

The Genealogy of Value in Classical Political Economy_

As my brief discussion of neoclassical economics in the previous chapter made clear, if we want to conceptually grasp the relation between capital and value (or between political economy and value), we cannot start with contemporary economics textbooks, because they have nothing to say about value.[1] Or, more accurately, what such textbooks do say about value can be boiled down to their rejections or disavowals of any role of or for value in economics. Of course, in order to broach the question of value we need not leave the history of economics entirely, since it is no exaggeration to say that the debate over value is the central debate in all of classical political economy, or to assert that the concept of value functions as the foundational *concept* for the

---

1 Throughout I treat "neoclassical economics" and "modern economics" as roughly synonymous. This is not because nothing has changed between the late nineteenth and early twenty-first centuries, but because the primary precepts of the "marginalist revolution" — which marked the fundamental break with the shared tenets of classical political economy — still reside at the core of the research program of the contemporary discipline of economics. As I hinted in the last chapter, this is not by accident, since, as Mirowski shows, the thread that ties them together is the suppression of value built into the basic equilibrium model (Mirowski 1989).

canonized classical thinkers. And, of course, modern economics still traces its own origins back to classical thinkers.

However, in order to treat the question of value as a serious one it its own right, this chapter's point of departure must be a thoroughgoing rejection of the selective and Whiggish history that modern economics offers. Neoclassical economics always proclaims (and/or pretends) that it rests on classical foundations, and contemporary textbooks never fail to give a shout out to Adam Smith. Here again, Paul Samuelson's textbook (Samuelson and Nordhaus 2010) is exemplary[2]: starting with a banal reference to *The Wealth of Nations* as "one of the greatest books of all economics" (16), it then asserts (falsely) that Smith was the first to recognize supply and demand forces[3] (28), proceeds to align the American Revolution's declaration of freedom with Smith's "emancipati[on] of trade and industry from the shackles of a feudal aristocracy" (29), and wraps it all up by first comparing Smith to Newton and then giving him (Smith) credit for being the first advocate of "economic growth" (30) — a concept that does not emerge until the 1940s (Allan 2018: 57).[4] It goes without saying that there is no mention whatsoever of Smith's primary contribution to classical political economy — namely, his arguments about value. But more to the point, these hagiographical references do nothing to explain the actual, historical relations between neoclassical and classical economic thought,

---

2 When it comes to the relation between Samuelson and the development (over the course of the twentieth century) of the neoclassical paradigm as a whole, Mirowski again provides helpful color: "Samuelson's role in the stabilization of the neoclassical orthodoxy is so monumental and far-reaching that it would be fair to say that we do not understand American neoclassicism until we can understand Samuelson" (Mirowski 1993: 342).

3 I'm not stepping out on a limb in calling this claim false. See https://en.wikipedia.org/wiki/Supply_and_demand#History.

4 In an important essay discussing Smith's role in the neoclassical paradigm, Mirowski concludes as follows: "it seems that the predominant value of our science is this faith in the 'natural' mechanism of the market and a 'natural progress' in the economic affairs of the race. It is this 'vision' of Smith that overcomes any other subsidiary failings in scientific values in the view of Western economists and places him in the hallowed position he occupies in the history of economic thought" (Mirowksi 1988: 207).

much less to contextualize the claims of the classical political economists.

Thus, in this chapter I take something like the opposite approach: rather than constructing a false line of progress, I chart the line of descent of economics — precisely the one that modern economics wishes to collapse or erase. More precisely, rather than conduct my own genealogy, here I propose to read Marx's *critique* of political economy as itself a genealogy of value in classical thought. To do so is to reconsider, simultaneously, the thinking of both Marx and classical political economy. By reading Marx as a genealogist of capitalist value, I reject constructions of him as an ahistorical economic theorist[5] or philosopher of human nature, and instead consider him as a theorist of the social formation[6] who makes it possible to grasp the form of

5   It is worth specifying that reading Marx as a genealogist means setting aside the problem of trying to get Marx's theory "correct" or to make it "consistent." These latter tasks, it seems to me, adequately capture the project of those committed to so-called temporal single-sector interpretation (TSSI) of Marx. Andrew Kliman has described his own recent synthetic contribution to the TSSI as "the most accessible full-length treatment of the controversy over Marx's *value theory* to date" (Kliman 2007: xv, emphasis added). I have italicized Kliman's reference to "value theory" to highlight the fact that, for the TSSI group, Marx's "value theory" is precisely an analytical, abstract, and timeless *economic theory* — not a genealogy of a complex and overdetermined social formation. The fact that Kliman wants to produce a consistent economic theory partially explains why he could write such a line in the preface to a book that does not *cite* any of the value-form theorists that I shall be discussing in my next chapter. Of course the value-form reading of Marx has its roots in Germany and thus in German-language texts, and TSSI is mainly an English-language theoretical development, but Kliman also fails to mention major English-language interpreters of Marx on value, such as Postone (1993) or Harvey (1982). None of this is meant as a substantive critique of TSSI, but merely as one explanation (along with the usual space and time constraints) of why I do not address it here.

6   In calling Marx a theorist of a "social formation," I allude to my own prior work on that concept, which I develop not directly from Marx but from an eclectic range of thinkers (including non-Marxists) (Chambers 2014). The idea of a social formation is one way to think the social whole in contradistinction to understandings of it as a system, a closed structure, or a totality. The social formation always remains open-ended and overdetermined. Contrary to notions often associated (perhaps not always fairly) with the

value that a capitalist social order produces and sustains. Specifically, through retracing Marx's own genealogy of classical political economy, we make it possible today to renew the question of the relation between value and a capitalist social order.

What is Value?_

Before turning to classical political economy, and in order to shorten our stay in the nineteenth century, I want first to ponder — perhaps rather abstractly — the question of value. At the outset I should restate a central point from the previous chapter: there are no distinct varieties or species of "value,"[7] nor do different types of value belong to distinct domains. To carry out a genealogy of value means to trace the emergence and transformation of value and value systems within a particular social order, which means to track them across the entirety of that society. Nietzsche, the first genealogist (at least in name), demonstrates this point conspicuously and powerfully. The transvaluation of values that he charts (and calls for) is bound up with ideas, theories, practices, and institutions that are political, cultural, religious, psychological, and economic. What Nietzsche

---

early Frankfurt School — particularly Horkheimer's famous statement that critical theory must take "society itself for its object" (Horkheimer 1999 [1937]: 206) — one can only think the social formation from within, and never in totalizing fashion. Contrary to a whole host of determinist Marxist accounts, the very structure of the social formation *precludes* linear causality, prediction, and determinism. See Chambers 2014.

7　Huber (2017) provides an illuminating contrast because he at first appears to reject my reading, yet ultimately his claims support it. In order to speak to environmentalists and to make Marx amenable to an audience that has taken him for a nature-dominating modernist, Huber asserts that there are two types of value — the sort that deals with capitalist exchange and the sort that deals with cultural worth (including that of the environment). But this opening move is a false feint, as Huber goes on to develop a reading of Marx in which the values of society are themselves produced, shaped, and constrained by the logic of capitalism: "under capitalism, no matter how much we might subjectively believe something has value, if it takes no labor to produce it, it will yield no value in the technical/economic sense" (Huber 2017: 44).

calls the "slave revolt in morality" cannot by any means be confined to a "moral realm," since this revolution in values starts with creditor–debtor relations, depends upon political transformations and war, and would not be possible without religious institutions — and this leaves out philosophers who, according to Nietzsche, have a central role to play in this transformation of values (Nietzsche 1967).

In turning here to the broad question of value, I do so with this genealogical context in mind. Following Nietzsche, while at the same time redeveloping Marx, I am always attempting to "bear society in mind," which in this case means to consider value as that society does. My fidelity to this approach explains why I eschew any call to come up with an a priori, technical, or analytical "definition" of value — one that I would then "apply" to particular situations or use as a foundation on which to build a model for the ideal account of value. Value's meaning is imminent to the social formation under discussion — whether it be late eighteenth-century Europe or early twenty-first-century America.[8]

One of the primary conundrums in interpreting the classical political economists on value is the simple fact that the very idea of value is utterly abstract and intangible; we cannot hold "value" in our hands, no matter how hard we try. The concept of value tempts us to grasp it generically, and thus to ignore Marx's own consistent striving for the historically concrete over the logically abstract. Marx understood, perhaps better than any

---

8 I have linked this approach to value with both the genealogical account and also Marx's particular and peculiar understanding of the historical development of social formations (see Chambers 2014), but my approach is not at all narrow or idiosyncratic, and there are other, viable and vibrant, intellectual sources for it. For example, taking as the meaning of value nothing other than the meaning of value as we encounter it in the world would be thoroughly consistent with a Wittgensteinian approach to meaning as emergent in the practice of language games. Value, on this account, has a "family resemblance" even across those language games (economics and moral philosophy) that would otherwise purport to keep the meanings separate (Wittgenstein 2009 [1953]). Sincere thanks to Bob Brecher for important dialogue on this point.

thinker before him, that "abstractions" are real in the sense that they are historically produced — and then they are *lived*. Therefore a first pass at "value" in an abstract sense may be just the thing we need to try to make the move that Marx called for — a shift from the always "chaotic conception" that is first given to us, to the "rich totality" that we can produce by working on that initial conception (Marx 1996 [1857]: 149).

How, then, do we understand value? There are a number of levels at which we talk about and think about value in everyday life. We can start with "subjective" value in the sense of the value to or for a subject: value as understood by an individual and in relation to that individual. "Subjective" here contrasts both with "objective" and "collective." Individuals *value* different things in different ways for different reasons; on this approach, "value" is thereby a result of the subjective human process of *valuing*.

Of course, subjective value is of use to us here mainly as a foil. In asking about value in terms of a larger social order, our interest lies *not* in value as gauged subjectively, because that sense of value tells us nothing about value systems, about the structure of value, or about value understood as a constitutive element of a social formation. Moreover, we can also say that the subjective process of valuation — the process by which a subject comes to have, hold, and articulate his or her values — always goes on against a thick background of already given "values." In other words, subjective value raises the question of value in some larger, broader, or systemic sense.

On a second pass, then, we might think of the background in which subjective values form in terms of those "cultural values" spoken of so commonly by anthropologists (or, perhaps more accurately, spoken of by *philosophers* in their questionable portrayal of anthropologists). We want to get at the very notion of a society's values: what a people or a time/place "values" prior to or regardless of the subjective valuation just discussed. I can personally value or not value patriotism, but if I live in the United States I cannot ignore the fact that, as a society, America today definitely does value patriotism — enormously so. Hence my dilemma upon buying a house (in 2015) with an already installed

20-foot-tall flagpole, from which the previous owners had flown an enormous American flag for many, many years. The flagpole looked extremely conspicuous with no flag flying, but to put up any flag other than (or at least, not including) the American flag would itself be just as conspicuous on a block in which at least five American flags are always visible from my front door. On the other hand, to take the flagpole down would itself be an easily detectable act, and one potentially subject to denouncement. Whatever values I might hold vis-a-vis flags and patriotism, my neighborhood holds a clear and palpable value system that I could not avoid or deny (Taylor 1985). The big question of value that we want to ask (and then answer) has to do with these broader, structural questions of value. Yet the general idea of "cultural values" cannot provide that sort of answer, since "cultural values" — the idea that values are the product and possession of a particular society in its specific time and place — will not get us beyond the thin anthropological idea I schematized above. The goal is to grasp values in a way that exceeds the notion that "society A values X and society B values Y." We want to know why, how, and on what grounds a society (usually our society, but potentially any) values whatever it values.

This brings us to a third sense of value, the very sense that answers the question of why a social order values what it values: "intrinsic value."[9] There are two simple ways that we might

9   In this context, Chris Arthur makes a crucial intervention when he points out something Marx knew quite well: one strand of classical political economy — most prominently, the work of Samuel Bailey — was devoted to a rejection of the very idea of value in itself with respect to commodity exchange. For Bailey, value in exchange is always utterly relative, always purely conjunctural; *it just so happens* that today three bananas are worth two apples, and tomorrow they are worth but one (Bailey 1825; Arthur 2004: 93). Arthur asserts that this argument has more bite to it than traditional Marxism has allowed. Neither Marx nor anyone else can establish a measure of value by merely *positing* it, and therefore saying — as Marx does early in the first chapter of the first volume of *Capital* — that in order for two commodities to be equal to one another they must both be equal to a "third thing," does not in itself prove the existence of an intrinsic value vis-à-vis commodities (Marx 1990: 127). Arthur's point is not that Marx's account of value fails, but that Marx's early, famous claim about the "third thing" serves

explain to ourselves why we value what we value. The first, addressed above, is to say "we just do" (Wittgenstein 2009; Oakeshott 1962); in other words, there is no further explanation for the values of a society. The second answer insists on the utter inadequacy of the first. "Intrinsic" value names the result of that process by which we go about explaining, *to ourselves*, our own cultural values. That is to say, our values are not relativistic because what we value has such value in itself. Value is not a result of our practices; we value things because they *are* valuable. In (re)constructing this logic, I am telling a story that explains so-called "cultural values" while refusing the simplistic (so-called anthropological) narrative of such values as *merely relative*. Within the terms of this narrative, we believe that something should be valuable in and of itself, and "cultural values" are just a (proper) reflection of this fact. Let me give a banal example: Americans would say that they value the equality of women and that the Taliban does not; "we" are right and "they" are wrong. Perhaps the better way of grasping this sense of value is to see that it deals with value at an ontological or metaphysical level. Value is a thing in and of the world, a part of human existence itself. "Intrinsic" value thereby points the way toward something quite significant for the overall engagement with value here: it helps us move away from subjective value without falling back on cultural relativism; it suggests the deeper structural truth of value for an entire social order.

Nothing I have said thus far would be inconsistent with textbook treatments of value in philosophy. Moreover, most of those discussions will explain value at the metaphysical level by deriving objective societal value from the more fundamental elements that make it up. This point is crucial: according to such a line of logic, *a social order has the value system it has because that system is taken as derived or deduced from the elements of value that society itself takes as fundamental*. Put another way, if

---

not to institute intrinsic value but rather to establish such an argument as necessary — an argument that only emerges later through Marx's unfolding of the value-form (as I will discuss in greater detail below).

society values families, if it prioritizes the sustenance and fosters the flourishing of families, if it structures institutions around the importance of families — then none of this should be thought of as purely arbitrary (to be contrasted with a society that does not value family). On the contrary, these value practices shall be cleaved to as a certain, logical deduction from the primary and fundamental value of family relations. For example, blood relations and the structure of a (nuclear) family become valued in society in particular ways precisely because the mother–child relation has a primary, elementary (i.e., intrinsic) value. The relation between parents and children is taken to be of fundamental importance; the relation between siblings is understood to be essentially of more value than a relation of friends (who can never be family). Such prior conditions *explain* a society's valuing of "family."[10]

) This particular example can of course be rightly seen as utterly contestable and/or full of contradictions. My point is not to defend or criticize the specific example of "family values," but to use it as a heuristic to explain the general structure whereby the cultural values of a society are understood as based upon elementary or natural foundations. Such an account refuses the idea that those values are "merely culture," and it stubbornly resists the notion that values are relative. Further, it accomplishes all this by fixing the social order's values on metaphysical moorings. The process amounts to tracing a social order's values back to their sources, but the sources themselves must not, by any means, be understood as products of that social order. Quite the opposite: the sources must be posited as fundamental, as elementary — this makes them metaphysically real or ontologically true.

---

10 In this particular example marriage becomes a crucial pivot since it enables non-blood relations to become family relations; marriage therefore must be understood as wielding a kind of sacred worth or power in order to shore up the intrinsic value of family (see Chambers 2009).

Capitalism and Value_

So what happens when we use this framework to think through the question of value in a capitalist society? That is, what ensues when we work out the problem of value within the specific context of a social formation that places the logic of capital at its center? First, I want to reiterate a crucial claim from the preceding chapter: the question of value within a capitalist regime (what Marx called "bourgeois society") is neither a random nor an ancillary idea, because the relation between value and capital is not arbitrary; *one of the things capitalism does is establish relations of value.* I will return to this decisive point, but first I want to consider the various ways that we might understand value under capitalism when using the schematic sketched in the previous section.

Capitalism tells us plainly that money and commodities are valuable; this is definitional. Indeed, capitalism establishes a powerful language of value in the shape of numerical monetary value. We know what things are worth in capitalism by looking at their price, and in the discourse of capitalist societies we all know that everything has its price. This means not only that capitalism provides a consistent, standardized framework for valuing, but also that anything that appears to fall outside of that framework can be translated back into it. Indeed, those of us who live in capitalist societies may often find it difficult to even pose the question of value because our social order makes it seem as if value is not a question: *value is a fact written on the surface of things, in the form of price.*

One simple way to understand the concept of marginal utility or the role of price theory in the program of neoclassical economics is to see them as displacing (or sublimating) the question of value. In the neoclassical model, marginal utility and/or marginal price come to stand in for value and render it putatively superfluous. This explains why the most important twentieth-century text on "value" speaks almost exclusively of *price* (Debreu 1959); as Mirowski helpfully puts it: "after Debreu, citations of value theory tend to use it as a synonym for price" (Mirowski 1989: 141).[11]

This translation — or perhaps better, transubstantiation — of value into price can be understood from two starkly contrasting, *yet ultimately complementary,* perspectives. On the one hand, if value *is* price/utility, then the question of value under capitalism no longer seems to be a question for artists, philosophers, novelists, or citizens; it is always and above all a question for economists and lawyers — and ultimately, for accountants. Value is located on the price tag, but if it cannot be easily found there, then it surely can be traced to the budget and tracked on the Excel spreadsheet. On the other hand, it is precisely when the neoclassical paradigm's equilibrium theory of one price replaces the earlier classical paradigm's explicit theories of value that we get the *bifurcation of value* into "economic value" and "moral value." The idea of moral value arises in response to the narrowing (if not evisceration) of value to price/utility; in the face of the theoretical futility and practical nihilism of rendering all value as price, capitalist social orders give rise to alternative theories of value (cf. Mirowski 1988: 100–101). But these are not

---

11   This claim curiously and conspicuously leaves out Maurice Dobb's *Theories of Value* and Distribution since Adam Smith (1973), a book which proves an important exception. I describe the exclusion in these terms because a reading of Dobb in parallel with Mirowski illuminates both authors covering much of the same ground and reveals a number of deep resonances between their distinct projects. First, on a general level both thinkers tell the story of the history of economics in terms of the displacement/repression of value theory effected by the marginalist revolution, and from the basis of this history, both thinkers relentlessly criticize the incoherence of the neoclassical paradigm. Second, to give one specific example, both Mirowski and Dobb go strikingly against the grain in describing Smith's theory of value as a stock, *not a labor,* theory of value. To be clear, Mirowski does cite Dobb (three times overall in the book), but he fails to identify Dobb as: 1) a mid-twentieth-century thinker who refuses to render value as a synonym for price; 2) a fierce critic of the neoclassical paradigm; and 3) an early interpreter of Smith as a "stock theorist" of value. In Mirowski's *Against Mechanism* (1988), published just one year before his major book *More Heat Than Light* (1989), he favorably refers to Dobb's 1937 volume, *Political Economy and Capitalism* (Mirowski 1988: 100).

alternatives to the neoclassical paradigm, per se; that is, they are not explanations of value that compete with the neoclassical account. They are, rather, accounts of value meant to apply to a different, non-economic domain, and thus to work alongside and in tandem with the neoclassical theory of economic value as price. Here we see in a more concrete sense how it might be possible — as I allusively suggested in the previous chapter — to think of the marginalist revolution as itself a potential (though surely not singular) cause of the idea that moral values and economic values are discrete entities.

To return to the schematic established in the previous section, we know that saying "within the neoclassical paradigm, value becomes price" is not a complete explanation, because an account of capitalist value cannot and must not be reduced to merely "capitalist value" in the relativistic sense — i.e., it cannot baldly assert that this is how value works under capitalism for no other reason than that a society is capitalist. As above, we still seek a deeper, non-relativistic explanation, one that roots our valuation system in something more substantial. There are two obvious candidates. The first is so commonsensical, so naturalized, that no one really even thinks of it in the way I have set it up — that is, as an answer to deep, metaphysical questions about intrinsic value. And the second is so much a product of rejected past history, that no one really remembers it or takes it seriously. Let me take each in turn.

Today, our intuitive understanding of value within capitalism depends on the fundamental idea that "the market" itself produces value.[12] This achievement — of explaining value as price

---

12 I should make clear early on that in referring to "intuitive" understandings I am not *opposing* intuition to other forms of knowledge. The problem I mean to identify lies not with our intuitions (which are just as reliable as any other senses and surely play an important role in understanding and knowledge), but with the way that classical political economy seeks to naturalize a capitalist social order by projecting its unique historical relations back onto a bogus pre-history, so as to render those relations ostensibly "intuitive" in a very problematic way. Indeed, from a different perspective we might say that it is our intuition that would first call our attention to the strangeness of the equation, three pairs of socks = one shirt, and Marx's critique of political

through market forces — is the hallmark of the neoclassical paradigm's equilibrium theory. Competition, the motor of the capitalist economy, is understood to create conditions in which all objects within the economy attain their true value. And market value stands in dramatic opposition to subjective valuation. I cannot decide the value of a loaf of bread: when I go to the store, the value of the bread is fixed, given — written legibly on the price tag. More to the point, the pure theory of microeconomic competition means that the grocer does not establish the value of the bread either: if she tries to sell too dearly, no one will buy from her and she will go out of business; if she sells too cheaply, she will not cover her costs, and again, she will go out of business.[13] The price of bread is determined by market powers themselves, established through the force by which "markets clear" when supply equilibrates demand. Value under capitalism is thus the height of objectivity; it comes not from any individual within the economic system, but is rather a complex achievement of the system itself. Just as the value of a loaf of bread can be objectively read off the price tag, so the true market value itself can be viewed at the point of intersection of the supply and demand curves.

---

economy seeks to mobilize precisely such intuitions. In other words, classical political economy before Marx can be understood as a project designed to naturalize a whole set of social arrangements that are anything but "intuitive." Thanks to Jane Bennett for spurring me on this point.

13   In a different context, I. I. Rubin nicely illuminates this exact phenomenon: "when he takes the final product of his labor to the market to exchange it, he is not free to determine the proportions of the exchange, but must submit to the conditions (the fluctuations) of the market, which are common to all producers of the given product. Thus, already in the process of direct production, he is forced to adapt his working activity (in advance) to the expected conditions of the market" (Rubin 2008 [1928]: 13). Notice that Rubin's point here goes beyond the one that I make in the text: not only can the grocer not dictate price, but the bread maker must engage in production with a market price already in mind. It was in this sense that Marx argued against the political economists' naive linear understanding of the economy, whereby production would always precede exchange: here we see the sense in which exchange can be "primary" and can condition production (Marx 1996: 139). I address Rubin in more depth in the following chapter.

The objectivity that I described above—that fundamental, rudimentary truth about value—is thus grounded in the fact of the market itself. Yet we tend *not* to think about the market as a metaphysical source for value; this is due to the consistent *naturalization* of market value. Capitalist value seems not to need metaphysical moorings because it appears so obvious, so undeniable. Commodities and money are valuable because the market says so: if Apple stock is trading at $110 per share, then it clearly must be *worth* $110 a share, since there is no other value given for it, and because no individual can alter that price. (One could of course choose to buy the stock at $120/share, but in that case one would be buying it not *at* its value but rather *above* its value; hence such an exception proves the rule.) Only the aggregation of all buyers and sellers of Apple stock, working through the magic of the market, can collectively (but non-intentionally) produce an outcome that changes the value of the stock. This is the power of the "invisible hand" metaphor, as it resonates with, but goes beyond, our subjectivist understandings of value. The hand writes the value of commodities directly onto them (through price), but is *invisible* since it is the hand of the market itself.

But what would it mean to think of value within a capitalist society in any other way? How could value *not* be understood as market price? Situations such as these, those in which it seems hard to think past or outside of our intuitive understandings, call for the work of genealogy. Genealogy moves backward in time, not to find the original source or putative truth of our present (not to locate an *Ursprung*), but instead to reveal a fractured line of descent (to pursue a *Herkunft*),[14] to expose the past as different and strange, and thereby ultimately to render the present contingent—to make it anything but inevitable.

In order to ask the question of capitalist value from a perspective other than our own, we can effectively turn to the work

---

14 Foucault's famous reading of Nietzsche on genealogy makes the distinction between *Ursprung* and *Herkunft* essential (Foucault 1984; Chambers 2001; cf. Cook 1990).

of the classical political economists.[15] They saw value under capitalism quite distinctly, because they approached capitalism differently. Where we take capitalism to be a given, a naturalized system that admits of no alternative, the classical political economists, even in their most ardent defense of capitalism, understand capitalism as something *new*, something particular and special. They see what we have a hard time seeing today: that capitalism is one among many different ways of ordering a society, and that capitalism's radical reorganization of the previous social order (feudalism) led to a revolutionary reconstruction of value systems.

The classical political economists came at the question of value in a manner that will surely strike us as odd, but the most important point is not their strangeness to us, but our strangeness to them. In requiring us to turn our attention to the past, the purpose of genealogy is not merely to make that past seem alien and unfamiliar, but rather to help us (or force us, as the case may be) to look *through* that past perspective, back toward the future — that is, our present — and to render it curious, even alien. In this way, genealogy can go beyond rendering the past foreign (a feat easily achieved anyway, as evidenced by most "period piece" movies) to producing a certain alterity of our own present. This, I think, is what Foucault meant by doing a "history of the present" (see Sedgwick 1990; Halperin 2002; Chambers 2009).

This is not at all to say that the classical political economists speak with a unified voice, but it is to affirm the extent to which

---

15 The most important authors in this tradition are surely nineteenth-century thinkers like Smith, Ricardo, Say, and Sismondi, but their debates can be connected to late seventeenth-century figures such as Petty and Boisguillebert. While one can make an important and convincing case that the early writers approached the very idea of political economy differently, that not until the nineteenth century did the abstract idea of the market and market forces become the central object of investigation of political economy (see Rebrovick 2016), Marx himself persuasively demonstrates the *links* between the earlier and later figures. Indeed, Marx shows that the thread that ties writers together across the two centuries is their shared attempt to solve the problem of value within a capitalist society.

they would all see our sense of capitalist value as failing to answer the fundamental question of where value comes from. For them, our answer — the market — would amount to no answer at all; it would appear as nothing other than bald-faced question-begging. Doubtless the classical economists grasped the power of markets, appreciated the mechanisms of supply and demand, and understood that markets both establish the equivalence of commodities and operate by way of monetary prices. They could easily perceive, just as plainly as we do, that markets establish value. However, *for them such a phenomenon was itself in need of explanation.* Again, this is certainly because for the political economists the mechanisms by which markets establish value were anything but given or natural: they were a radically new, *historical* development established by massive technological, social, and political change. The system by which the logic of capital established value did not have the imprimatur of objective truth for the classical political economists, and therefore they set out to give it the metaphysical moorings that it lacked. Where, they queried, does the value of commodities come from? How, they asked, could we trace market value to a more fundamental, underlying value?

Today we simply see no need to ask such questions; the mainstream profession of economics has not asked them for over a century. Nonetheless, the classical political economists shared with us the fundamental sense that a society's value system needed to be based on genuine, stable foundations. But here lies the key twist: for the classical political economists the market itself could not serve as that foundation (as it does for us today), because for them, the market did not yet have the metaphysical reality that it attained in the twentieth century.[16] Therefore, for thinkers from the seventeenth through the nineteenth centuries, the question of the value of commodities needed to be answered

---

16   As Tripp Rebrovick shows, the market had a reality and a certain force for the classical political economists, yet it was not a substantive, circumscribed domain, and it did not have metaphysical depth; moreover, the "economy" as a domain of existence in the way we understand it today, had not yet come into being (Rebrovick 2016).

by finding some element of *intrinsic* worth that could explain the value of commodities as they operated under (i.e., according to) the logic of capital. Political economy as a field was forged in the fierce debates over the question of value, with most centering on "labor" as a potential answer. Entire schools of thought and diverse political projects were born in the process of trying to understand what labor is and how it might be that labor could constitute the essence of value within a capitalist social order. In this context, I now turn to Marx.

Marx as Genealogist_

Marx matters for me here, first of all, because of his genealogical work. Marx followed the descent of classical political economy, showing how the answer to the value question changed, shifted, was reworked, faced challenges, and was reformulated over the course of almost two hundred years of political economy. At the start, let me clarify the status of genealogy in my project. I want to call attention to the *genealogical work* that Marx does in relation to classical political economy and to use a certain reading of him *as* a genealogist to draw out the stakes of his self-titled *critique* of the political economists. In short, treating Marx as if he were a genealogist reveals a great deal that is otherwise occluded in other approaches to Marx, and in certain contexts, we see clearly that he operates as a genealogist — that is, according to the precepts and methods of genealogy as later outlined by Nietzsche, Foucault, and their readers. But my point is not to "make" Marx into a genealogist, or to contend that all of his writings should be read this way. Marx wore many hats when he wrote: historian, journalist, polemicist, pamphleteer, and economic pedagogue; it would be at best naive to think all those roles could be contained under the heading of genealogy. Moreover, there can be no doubt that Marx's presentation of his critique of political economy in *Capital* looks far less genealogical than that in the earlier writings on which I focus. I intend not to deny that difference, but to highlight it, and along the way to show that we learn a great deal from the genealogical Marx of the 1850s that might otherwise be missed in the much more famous (and less genealogical) published writings of the 1860s.[17]

My broadest contention is that it would prove impossible to make sense out of, much less evaluate or judge, any answer that Marx himself might have given to the question of value, without first laying out his detailed and precise description and criticism of those answers that had recently preceded him in political economy. This claim would hold even if one's primary aim was to uncover Marx's own answer: Marx says over and over again—he repeats it throughout his writings over a long span of time—that his account of capitalism emerges out of his engagement with political economy. Yet, in some ways this

---

17 The above calls for two ancillary elaborations. First, some writers would explain Marx's move from the 1850s to the 1860s in terms of a shift from his "transitional works" to his "mature works" (Althusser 1965), while others would explain all of Marx's developments as a march toward "science" (Engels, along with countless twentieth-century Marxists). I accept that Marx changed his presentation, sometimes quite significantly, but I reject the idea that he did so in order to make that presentation more "scientific." Quite to the contrary, the evidence from Marx's letters and other writings indicates that, above all else, Marx desired to make the presentation in *Capital* as *clear as possible* for the widest possible audience, and not at all to make it "more scientific." Marx's desire to make himself understood as broadly as possible marks his work from early to late; see, for example, the clarifications of Marx's presentation of early drafts of *Capital* in his talk "Value, Price and Profit" (1995). Ultimately, of course, Marx thought that the best way of presenting his discoveries about capitalism was not through genealogy; hence, my clarification in the text above to the effect that reading Marx as a genealogist should not at all be confused with the notion that Marx himself meant to be a genealogist. None of this changes the basic fact that the emphasis on science surely comes after Marx, and while not all of the blame can be laid at Engels's feet, a great deal of it surely can (Carver 2003: chap. 6; cf. Arthur 2004). Second, a delimited reading of Marx as a genealogist opens up a number of avenues for fruitful comparison and contrast with much more famous genealogical thinkers—namely, Nietzsche and Foucault. In order to make the case that one can read Marx this way, I point to some of the comparisons, below, but I would not want to diminish the differences. In particular, both Nietzsche and Foucault propose something like an "art of the self," a creative and transformative *ethos* that plays no real part in Marx's thought. Thanks to Bill Connolly and Patrick Giamario for help on this last point.

understates the point. We might do better to put it this way: Marx's delineation of the logic of capital *is his critique of political economy*. Here I paraphrase Marx, who, in a famous line from a letter, once described his work-in-progress on capital by referring to it as "the system of bourgeois political economy critically presented," and in case that were not clear enough, Marx continued "it is the *Darstellung* of the system and, at the same time, through the *Darstellung*, its *Kritik*" (Marx and Engels 1963; quoted in Carver 1975: 28–29). I leave the German in the quotes to emphasize the way in which, for Marx, the "presentation" is intimately bound up with "critique." Furthermore, the *Darstellung* here is not simply a direct "presentation" or "description" of the precepts of classical political economy, but also a "representation," a "production"—perhaps even a "performance," of Marx's own thought.

I am not the first to make the case that Marx cannot be understood outside of the context of his critical engagement with classical political economy. The claim is commonplace, and few readers of Marx would deny the obvious facts: that he read the classical political economists closely and carefully, and that he developed his own understanding of capitalism through, and in distinction to, their works. Nonetheless, aside from a general gesture in the direction of Smith and Ricardo, it is surprising how rarely the fact of Marx's engagement with political economy actually shapes or influences interpretations of Marx. As Michael Heinrich helpfully shows, Marx's own plan for the project named *Capital* was to write four total books — three theoretical, and one on the history of political economy. Marx's historical work was therefore not just preparatory to the production of *Capital*, but essential to the work itself. Heinrich argues that the missing history book "would not have been just an addendum to the three theoretical books; it would probably have been an important key to a better understanding of the theoretical arguments themselves" (Heinrich 2009: 89). I follow Heinrich when I argue that to read Marx as a genealogist is not to hive off his genealogical thought from his analytical or critical or theoretical or scientific work, but to illuminate more brightly his entire project.

How, exactly, does one connect the *Darstellung* of political economy to the *Kritik* of the logic of capital? Put differently, what does it mean, concretely, to read Marx as a genealogist? The answer is (at least) two-fold: we need to *read Marx differently* and we need to *read different texts* of Marx. In the first instance, this means approaching Marx as a genealogist, by assuming that his project cannot stand separately on its own, as a linear account built on a slab foundation. Marx's ideas emerge in critical dialogue with the political economists, whose ideas he not only criticizes but also praises and further develops. In the second instance, this means focusing our attention on those texts where Marx himself most strikingly foregrounds the political economists.

This is precisely why I turn here to a text of Marx's in which he does much more than mention political economy generally, a work wherein Marx provides his own focused genealogy of classical political economy. I center my reading on Marx's published work of 1859, *Zur Kritik der Politischen Ökonomie*, which appears half a century later in English as *A Contribution to the Critique of Political Economy* (1904).[18] This book has been doubly eclipsed: first by *Capital* and then by the so-called *Grundrisse* (both of which, in a way, "contain" *Zur Kritik* in their own ti-

---

18 Unlike many of the more famous "works by Marx," such as the *Economic and Philosophic Manuscripts, The German Ideology*, and *The Grundrisse* (see Carver and Blank 2014a; 2014b; cf. Heinrich 2009: 77), Marx himself published *Zur Kritik*. This might suggest that Marx was more concerned with publishing material that engaged with the political economists, while twentieth-century editors were more interested in contributing to "Marxism." Putting that larger point aside, it should be noted that Marx also gives a genealogical-like presentation in *Theories of Surplus Value* (1969a; 1969b), where he again works through the classical political economists one by one. However, this later work places the political economists into little boxes that Marx has already worked out; it reads more like a post hoc summary. As I see it, the 1859 text holds an advantage, because there we witness Marx engaging these thinkers while still discovering his own position, and so, in short, he offers a much more thorough *reading* in this earlier text and the reader experiences a much richer *encounter*.

tles[19]). The latter text is often *presumed* to be more saturated by Hegelian philosophy than it is engaged with classical political economy,[20] while the former work removes, or confines to the footnotes,[21] most of the direct evidence of that very engagement.

---

19   That is, in literal terms, "the critique of political economy" — to which *Zur Kritik* is a contribution — is the subtitle of *Capital*, and the very thing that the *Grundrisse* outlines or sketches. The former text would seem to be the definitive, published presentation of Marx's critique of political economy, while the latter — in its size and scope and serious entwinement with Hegelian thought — would seem to be the widest and deepest presentation. *Capital* thus swallows up *Zur Kritik* in its subtitle, while the *Grundrisse* displaces *Zur Kritik* in its reification of the untranslated German word for "outlines." For more historical and conceptual discussion on treating the *Grundrisse* as a book of Marx's, if not *the* book of Marx's, in its own right, see Chambers 2014; Rosdolsky 1977. For the historical argument that *Capital* and the "critique of political economy" were actually *separate* projects, see Heinrich 2009: 85.

20   I reject the common presumption of a binary between Marx's interest in Hegel (understood as Hegelian *philosophy*) and his interest in political economy. As Carver forcefully argues, "Marx's detailed interest in Hegel was precisely in his [Hegel's] 'political economy'"; moreover, "'Hegelian philosophy' isn't intellectual or politically 'other' to Marx's detailed engagement with political economists, who aren't themselves absent in Hegel's work" (Terrell Carver, email to author, October 2016). My point in the text above is therefore not to reify such a binary, but merely to invoke its very real existence in the secondary literature on Marx, as a partial explanation for why the interpretive attention paid to the *Grundrisse* has sometimes come at the expense of careful analysis of Marx's own readings of the classical economists. Of course, a strain of value-form theory (discussed in the next chapter) has carefully articulated a more rigorous and subtle relation between Hegel's dialectical logic (as distinguished from a dialectical account of history) and Marx's analysis of the logic of capital (see Arthur 2004).

21   The distance between Marx's presentation of value and the commodity in *Zur Kritik* and that in *Capital* can be significantly reduced if one pays careful attention to the footnotes to chapter 1 of *Capital*. There Marx preserves the running commentary on the classical political economists, and he emphasizes over and over the importance of the value-form. Indeed, and as I will discuss in much greater detail below, the standard reading of Marx as signing on to a (version of) the Labor Theory of Value depends upon ignoring the footnotes, since this is the place where Marx quite clearly delineates the insufficiency of such a theory. It is worth noting that these are some of the longest, most substantive footnotes in Marx's entire oeuvre. For a distinct but complementary reading that also emphasizes these notes, see Bidet 2007: 52.

Zur Kritik hits the sweet spot: it retains a sharp focus on — and for the most part, only on — the work of classical political economy. *Zur Kritik* also proves that in developing his understanding of the logic of capital, Marx never started over from scratch or sought a *tabula rasa*; he advanced his understanding of capital *through* an engagement with the work of classical political economy. The best evidence here is surely the extent to which the opening chapter of the first volume of *Capital* closely tracks the first chapter of *Zur Kritik* (see Rubin 2008). *Zur Kritik* provides numerous examples of Marx's own embeddedness in specific works of the political economists: places where, if one looks closely, it is possible to see the text Marx was reading when he wrote specific lines in his own manuscript. Indeed, the exercise of reading Smith, Ricardo, and *Zur Kritik* in succession is itself enough to make an interpreter of Marx completely rethink what is going on in the opening chapters of *Capital*.

Here I want to narrow my focus by analyzing an entire section of *Zur Kritik* that has no presence at all in *Capital*. *Zur Kritik* begins almost exactly as *Capital* does: in both books, chapter 1 is titled "The Commodity," and the opening sentence of the latter book is only a slight extension of the exact same sentence in the former book. Many have analyzed the subtle historical and textual details of the evolution of Marx's thought over the course of the various versions of this chapter, but the most glaring difference between *Zur Kritik* and *Capital* appears at the end of the chapter: where *Capital* moves straight to chapter 2, *Zur Kritik* contains a rather odd supplement in the form of a section titled "Historisches zur Analyse der Ware."

English translations of *Zur Kritik* have not known quite what to do with this section. In the original German, the section appears as an organic part of the chapter, marked off with the lettered heading "A," but otherwise integrated into chapter 1. And a section titled "Historical Analysis of the Commodity" (a literal translation, but also a straightforwardly obvious one to choose) seems a fitting continuation of a chapter on "the commodity." Indeed, as I will argue, it provides just the needed, clarifying genealogical context for Marx's critical presentation of the commodity in the earlier parts of the chapter. On my reading of Marx — not just in this text, but as a whole — the historical analysis of commodities is essential to any contemporary understanding of commodities within a capitalist social order. Commodities are not timeless objects, nor are they the elementary building blocks of a capitalist system; commodities are historical productions of capitalism, at the very same time as they provide the conditions of possibility for capitalism itself. The *Darstellung* of the history of commodities is therefore the *Kritik* of the capitalist logic that circulates commodities.

But this is not at all how the English translations present this section. Most acutely, both translations change the title of the section in a way that marks it as supplemental, perhaps even unnecessary. The more recent, 1970 translation by Ryazanskaya (Marx 2009) — widely available through the *marxists.org* website — comes closest to the German with its "Historical Notes on the Analysis of Commodities." It thus does far better than the original Stone translation (Marx 1904), which bizarrely renders the section title, "Notes on the History of the Theory of Commodities" — somehow suggesting that Marx meant *Theorie* when he wrote *Analyse*. In any case, the appearance of a "historical notes" heading at the end of chapter 1 clearly signals to the reader that the section is ancillary, appendix-like. The heading says that what follows are merely historical footnotes to the primary work undertaken in the main body of the chapter. Indeed, the online version of the Ryazanskaya translation actually places the section *after the endnotes* from chapter 1.[22] At best, such a presentation tempts the reader to approach the section like so many of Marx's "notebooks" from the same period (at worst, it tells the reader to skip this section entirely). Those notebooks included outlines and sketches of engagements with other authors that Marx himself eventually discarded in favor of his fi-

---

22 The online German version of the text integrates the "Historical Analysis" section into the main body of the chapter, and it places all endnotes together at the end of each chapter. The paperback version of the Stone translation uses running footnotes.

nal, published formulation. The problem with this framing is obvious, however, since unlike the so-called *1844 Manuscripts*, or the *Grundrisse*, or *The German Ideology* — all texts that were published after Marx's death, and that in most cases were editorial constructions, not "books Marx wrote" — *Marx himself published Zur Kritik* in his own lifetime (Carver and Blank 2014a). We thus have every reason to believe that this section at the end of chapter 1 contains material that Marx thought was essential to the argument, not preparatory or auxiliary. In the terms I have been developing here, this would mean that Marx saw his genealogical analysis of political economy's treatment of the commodity as central to his own conceptual articulation of the commodity within a capitalist social formation. Hence I will now trace the historico-analytic map that Marx draws, thereby starting with his genealogy, rather than with his more abstract and decontextualized presentation of "the commodity" as it appears both at the beginning of *Zur Kritik* and also in the various editions of *Capital*.

The Genealogy of Capitalist Value_

While Marx titles this section at the end of chapter 1 of *Zur Kritik*, "Historical Notes on the Analysis of Commodities," the focus of his investigation is better captured by the 1904 translation's helpful *mis-titling* of the section in its table of contents as "Notes on the History of the Theory of Value." Factually, this entry in the table of contents is simply wrong, but substantively it holds a lot of truth, since Marx's main goal in this portion of the chapter seems to be less to sort through the political economists' broad understandings of the commodity, and more to home in on their specific sense of the relation between three terms/objects within capitalism: value, the commodity, and labor. For Marx, there is something of a progress narrative to be told in charting the history of political economy from the late seventeenth to the mid-nineteenth century: as each theorist builds from the work of his predecessors and quarrels with his contemporaries, so he comes closer to getting something *right* about this relationship, and thus closer to grasping the very nature of value under capitalism. Thus, Marx's genealogy can itself be boiled down to a series of theses defended by the various political economists, each of which asserts the relationship between value and commodities in terms of labor.

Marx starts with Petty,[23] and lest my above description make it sound as if Marx imposes a teleological structure to his chronological account of the results of political economy, I should call attention to Marx's emphasis that it is Petty, writing a century before Smith, who first lays claim to the central importance of "division of labor" as productive of material wealth. In Marx's eyes, Petty's work is important, and genuinely deserving of the title of "political economy...as a separate science," because Petty, unlike "his contemporary Hobbes," sees that within an emerging bourgeois social formation, value can be produced in a way that is *not* determined by "natural factors" (Marx 2009 [1859]: 22).[24] For Marx this means that commodity value has a "*social aspect*" — the importance of which absolutely cannot be underestimated. In specifying this dimension, Marx indicates to his readers that we must trace the value of a commodity not

---

23 Readers of Marx all know that Marx commonly references Smith and Ricardo, but Marx's engagement with the field of political economy went much deeper than these, the most famous English political economists, and it extended back much earlier than his nineteenth-century contemporaries. Marx opens this section of *Zur Kritik* by referring to "the decisive outcome of the research carried on for over a century and a half by classical political economy," starting with the work of Petty and Boisguillebert in the seventeenth century.

24 All my citations are to the Ryazanskaya translation of *Zur Kritik*. The 1979 Progress Publishers edition of the book is out of print, while the online version hosted at the Marxists Internet Archive is updated and freely available. However, the widely read version hosted at Marxists.org has no page numbers (or paragraph or section numbers). My in-text references are therefore to a PDF version of that edition, which includes page numbers. It is available from the Internet Archive, here: https://archive.org/details/MarxContributionToTheCritiqueOfPoliticalEconomyClean. In instances where I have modified the translation myself I have drawn from the *Marx-Engels-Werke* (MEW) (Marx and Engels 1971). There is an accessible online version of *Zur Kritik* in German available as well: http://www.mlwerke.de/me/me13/me13_015.htm.

to something physically inherent or naturally integral to the object itself, but rather to something about the larger social order that would produce, distribute, exchange, and consume such commodities (Marx 2009: 115, emphasis added; cf. Murray 1999; Murray 2000).[25] Petty, however, makes a mistake common to his day, and in a distinct way, even to our own: "he accepts exchange-value as it *appears* in the exchange of commodities" (Marx 2009: 22). Much like we do today, Petty sees market value as the truth of value, but more to the point, in Petty's own time period, to assume the truth of market value was to mistakenly take gold itself for value. Of course, as I underlined above, all of the political economists share the goal of going outside of market exchange itself in order to locate the source of market (i.e., commodity) value. In Petty's case, that means finding value literally in gold. And here Petty can only resort, according to Marx,[26] to locating the value of gold (and thus of all commodities) within "the particular kind of concrete labor by which gold" is mined from the earth (Marx 2009: 22). In other words, for Petty, the source of market value is exchange, which depends upon gold, and the source of gold's value is the labor of mining. Marx does not even bother to say to the reader explicitly how nonsensical he finds such a conclusion; general value under capitalism cannot be traced to any one, specific type of concrete labor (there is no magical property of mining for gold).

---

25 In the first chapter of *Zur Kritik* Marx places enormous emphasis on social labor. And in exactly this context, Marx makes it clear that the "reduction" of value to abstract labor is not a philosophical reduction (or a philosophical abstraction), not a reduction that a thinker or writer carries out; it is a real reduction (and a real abstraction). Marx writes: "This reduction *appears* to be an abstraction, but it is an abstraction *which is made every day in the social process of production* (Marx 2009: 8, emphasis added). In the French edition of the first volume of *Capital*, Marx emphasizes that "only exchange brings about this reduction" (quoted in Rubin 2008: 149).

26 My aim is to recapture Marx's genealogical re-presentation of political economy, not myself to reconstruct the political economists' work; therefore, all of my descriptions above are readings of *Marx* on the particular political economists. I have no doubt that Marx's own presentations may contain their own idiosyncrasies.

Boisguillebert sees the other side of the coin (no pun intended), as he recognizes that exchange-value cannot be traced to any concrete labor practices, but must instead be understood in terms of an abstract labor-time. This is a great advance in grasping value under capitalism, but as Marx reads him, Boisguillebert remains hopelessly confused because he cannot clearly perceive the difference between, on the one hand, the production of commodities for exchange (the production of use-values for exchange, use-values understood in terms of their exchange-value — i.e., capitalist production), and, on the other hand, the direct production of use-values as a "material substance of wealth, its use-value, enjoyment of it" (Marx 2009: 22). Marx portrays Boisguillebert as trapped in the Old World, wishing to affirm bourgeois labor (the labor that produces commodities as exchange-values) while railing against bourgeois forms of wealth (particularly money).

The breakthrough in grasping bourgeois relations could only come from a (naive) New World man. Marx credits Benjamin Franklin with nothing less than "formulat[ing] the basic law of modern political economy...he declares it necessary to seek another measure of value than the precious metals, and [he asserts] that this measure is labor" (Marx 2009: 23). Franklin frees himself from the temptation to think of value in terms of gold and silver, and this enables him to establish not a natural or universal law (not even a law of capitalism), but a *law of political economy*. Franklin was the very first to "deliberately and clearly (*so clearly as to almost be trite*) reduce exchange-value to labor time" (Marx 2009: 23, emphasis added).

What does it mean to call this a "reduction" (a "trite" one at that) and what sort of force could effect this reduction — the force of Franklin or Marx's words, or that of capital itself? To arrive at an answer, Marx must first bring into view what Franklin misses. Marx treats Franklin as an "idiot savant," who was never taken seriously as a political economist and did not influence the field directly. Franklin thus fails to perceive the potential breakthrough offered by his own deep insight into capitalist exchange. Nevertheless, Franklin grasps the fundamental fact that capitalist exchange is effectively the exchange of quantities of labor for other quantities of labor, and therefore the only *possible* measure of value within capitalism is labor-time. The question Franklin thereby brings to the fore (without himself realizing it) is the key question for Marx: *what type of labor is exchanged in capitalism* — and relatedly, how does a bourgeois social order make such exchange possible in the first place?

Franklin himself cannot answer this question because he has no sense whatsoever of production: as Marx puts it, "the transformation of actual products into exchange-values is taken for granted." Franklin therefore cannot grasp the transformation — the *revolution* — in production wrought by capitalism (Marx 2009: 23).[27] More importantly, Franklin's blindness to the transformative effects of a bourgeois social order also prevents him from coming to a deeper understanding of labor. Like Smith, as we will see below, Franklin is tempted by the notion that labor is, or partakes of, some essence; this would make labor itself, in the form of "labor-time," the source of value because of the essential nature of labor. Marx will subtly suggest something radically different: that "labor itself" should really always be understood as "labor under capitalism," or labor under a particular type of social order. In other words, there is no such thing as labor *itself*, but only labor as it operates within a particular social order.

Marx articulates this claim — subtly at first, and then more forcefully — by referring to a particular type of object, an object produced by a capitalist social formation (Chambers 2014: 2–8). We can pick out this profound point in Marx's reading of Franklin by taking care to note the conceptual and termino-

---

27 More than any other thinker of this time period, Marx stresses the fact that what really changes under capitalism is not the general idea of market exchange, but the fundamental nature of production — *production for market exchange*. This does not make Marx a so-called "productivist" thinker in the essentialist sense of positing human beings as uniquely "productive" creatures. Marx's point is genealogical: the nature of the social organization of production under capitalism is what makes a capitalist social formation unique (see Wood 2016).

logical work that Marx does here, yet to bring the claims out clearly we will need to work our way past what the English translations might unintentionally obscure. In his most forceful concluding remarks, Marx tells his reader that Franklin "fails to see the intrinsic connection between money," on the one hand, and *Tauschwert setzende Arbeit*, on the other (Marx 2009: 23). What is *Tauschwert setzende Arbeit*, and how is it intrinsically connected to money? The phrase is hard to render in smooth English because in it labor (*Arbeit*) is modified by both the noun "exchange-value" (*Tauschwert*) and the present participle "positing" (*setzende*) (Marx and Engels 1971). A literal translation would thus be "exchange-value-setting-labor" or "exchange-value-positing-labor."

I will return to the question of translation shortly, but first I want to clarify that throughout *Zur Kritik* Marx repeatedly refers to *Tauschwert setzende Arbeit* as the unique historical production of a bourgeois society. Only under capitalism does this particular element, *Tauschwert setzende Arbeit*, make its first appearance. As I read Marx, he wishes to underscore the novelty of this production and to emphasize its historical specificity. Therefore, rather than saying that labor (a transhistorical force) takes on new features or gains new capacities, Marx argues instead that through complex historical development a completely new type of object emerges, and that object is *Tauschwert setzende Arbeit*. The phrase appears over and over again throughout the entirety of the book; one could even argue that *the conceptual innovation* of *Zur Kritik* must be located here, with Marx's discovery of *Tauschwert setzende Arbeit* as the unique object produced by a capitalist social order.

With this in mind, one can consider the translation. The multiple hyphens of the literal translation, exchange-value-setting-labor, is ungainly, and so one can easily understand why the English translators looked for alternatives that would scan better. Ryazanskaya chooses "labor which posits exchange value" and Stone picks "labor which produces exchange value." In an overall functional sense, neither translation is wrong: both translations have Marx, in his discussion of Franklin, comparing two objects — money, on the one hand, and a unique type of labor, on the other. That is, in English "labor which posits" or "labor which sets" exchange value is still itself a grammatical object. Nonetheless, the English translations have made a subtle change that matters: in order to create a smoother-reading English prose, these translations sacrifice a crucial element of Marx's conceptualization and they make it easier to miss or to misread one of the central points of his account. The translations have substituted for the German participle *setzende* the English phrase "which sets" (or "which posits"). That is, rather than go directly to an English participle, "setting," the translations give a relative pronoun, "which," followed by a present tense verb, "sets." All of this matters because it places an active verb (*sets* or *posits*) in the center of the phrase, giving the false appearance of labor functioning as an active force,[28] rather than portraying it as a particular kind of object produced by a bourgeois society.

Readers of the English translation can thus easily lose a sense of the very specific, highly particular *type of object* Marx is delineating here: exchange-value-positing-labor, or exchange-value-producing-labor. The difference is not merely semantic. Rather than identifying particular capacities that a generic labor has (to do certain things or achieve particular ends), and rather than describing a distinct aspect or property of labor itself, Marx is pointing to the *unique type* of labor under capitalism. In this sense the awkwardly hyphenated term proves to be utterly appropriate, since the hyphens (in English) call attention to the distinct, peculiar nature of this object, an object that can only

---

28 This is not to deny that the English participle ("setting" or "positing," in this case) also takes on the verb form, but as a contemporary grammar guide explains, a participle is a verb form functioning as an adjective. Moreover, the "-ing" form of the participle also operates, in the case of gerunds, as a noun, and it functions as a verb only in the progressive tense — a tense that is much less direct and active than the present tense that appears in the English translation (CCCF 2016). To boil this down: "setting-labor" *sounds like* some very odd or downright bizarre object, while "labor which sets" sounds like a description of labor doing something. The former sense, I argue, is exactly what Marx had in mind, while the latter is not even close.

come into existence within the precise conditions and environment of a capitalist social formation.

This conclusion needs to be underscored: capitalist labor proves to be a strange sort of labor. It is for just this reason that there can be what Marx calls an "intrinsic connection" — the connection Franklin thoroughly misses — between money and the type of labor we see in capitalism, exchange-value-positing-labor. To claim such an inherent link between money and exchange-value-setting-labor means not only to reject the simplistic notion that money would somehow be naturally tied to "labor itself" but also to refute the standard account of money — the orthodox theory still repeated by economics textbooks today and echoed by Franklin himself in 1731, in a text that was titled *A Modest Inquiry into the Nature and Necessity of a Paper Currency.* As Marx reads him, Franklin "regards money as a convenient technical device which has been introduced into the sphere of exchange from outside" (Marx 2009: 23). Today's textbooks say much the same thing when they account for money as an efficient lubrication of (natural) exchange — a facilitation of a barter process itself thought to be autochthonous. In contrast, Marx here is implying that money is not at all a convenience, not a technical advance that facilitates functions already inherent to human interaction. Rather, money *does* have an inherent connection to the type of object uniquely produced by a capitalist social formation — namely, exchange-value-positing-labor. Money, Marx hints here, is the form that value takes, and *must take*, under capitalism.[29]

---

29 What Marx calls the *intrinsic* connection between money and exchange-value-setting-labor serves as powerful evidence of Marx's significant departure from what Geoffrey Ingham helpfully labels the orthodox theory of money (Ingham 2004). Ingham faults Marx for the latter's commodity-centric account of money, but Ingham fails to note Marx's clear rejection of the "neutral veil" thesis of orthodox theory. The latter is quite content to describe a "real economy" that does without money entirely. Such a notion came to flourish after Marx, but he himself would have scoffed at it. For Marx, there is no such thing as a capitalist social formation without money, since money is itself the *necessary* form of appearance of value under capi-

Before fully addressing that idea, Marx continues his genealogy by showing his readers that many of the political economists writing after Franklin continue to pursue an understanding of capitalist value, which we can now describe in terms of distinctly capitalist labor, by traveling down dead-ends. A number of thinkers simply formulate the question incorrectly, à la Petty, by asking "what particular kind of concrete labor is the source of bourgeois wealth" (Marx 2009: 23–24). The terms I delineated earlier reveal why this is a malformed question: the source of value within a capitalist social order cannot be any particular form of concrete labor. The source can only be abstract labor, exchange-value-positing-labor, but one must not confuse abstract labor as the form of labor that emerges within capitalism with any specific variety of concrete labor practices. These thinkers are digging in the wrong place, looking for the source of value where it can never be found.[30] This explanatory structure provided by Marx helps makes sense of the Physiocrats' claim that the primary source of value is wheat or corn (*blé*) and that therefore the concrete labor that produces value can only be agricultural labor.[31] And it leads Marx to a piercing

---

talism (Murray 1993; Moseley and Campbell 1997). I take up this discussion in more detail in the next chapter.

30 Mirowski argues convincingly that for the classical political economists, the dominant scientific metaphor was not Newtonian laws and action at a distance, but Cartesian space, causality, and substance. For Mirowski, what holds classical political economy together is the shared understanding of "the Cartesian conception of value as a physical substance," and to this end he credits Smith, with his insistence on "'primary and elementary objects,'" as the great-yet-unheralded Cartesian (Mirowski 1989: 163–64, quoting Smith 1869: 386). I disagree entirely with Mirowski's reading of Marx, yet I find his overall account of classical political economy enormously helpful in illuminating the ways that Marx takes the paradigm of a substantialist account of value as his precise object of critique. Mirowski identifies the paradigm eloquently, but he misses the fact that Marx works not only in it but also *against it*.

31 Marx stresses, however, that what really matters most for the Physiocrats, and in this their work forms an invaluable resource for Marx's own thinking, "was not what kind of labour creates *value* but what kind of labour creates *surplus value*." Marx thus gives the Physiocrats a pass when it comes to his main critical point in this text — that no concrete labor can be the

critique of claims like those of Steuart, who tries to locate the ultimate source of all value in precious metals, in "the silver in the silver filigree, its '*intrinsic worth*'" (Marx 2009: 24, quoting Steuart 1767: 361). We might understand these blunt, empiricist answers — "empiricist" because they seek the intrinsic value of commodities in some concrete substance — as products of the period of transition: these thinkers hold on to feudal understandings of wealth while trying to make sense of the newly emerging concept of value under capitalism.

Despite his confusions, Steuart, Marx tells us, also sees through the fog to reach some striking insights. Steuart benefits from being able to witness the *emergence* of a capitalist social order, allowing him to observe the "*difference* between bourgeois and feudal labor" (Marx 2009: 24, emphasis added). Marx thereby derives a powerful insight from Steuart: "the commodity as the elementary and primary unit of wealth, and alienation as the predominant form of appropriation are characteristic only of the bourgeois period of production, so exchange-value-positing-labor is specifically bourgeois" (Marx 2009: 24, translation modified). Marx again returns to the phrase *Tauschwert setzende Arbeit*, but here he goes further to underscore the point that exchange-value-positing-labor belongs in particular to a capitalist social order. It is *specifically bourgeois*.

At this stage in his genealogy Marx grows more emphatic: the idea of labor creating, producing, or positing exchange-value is not a metaphysical truth — it is not something intrinsic to labor itself.[32] Exchange-value-setting-labor is bourgeois labor — labor

---

source of value — because he admires the Physiocrats for glimpsing the importance of surplus value (even if in "contradictory form") (Marx 2009: 24). In this context, Rubin powerfully illuminates the importance of capitalist structures for the Physiocrats: "when the Physiocrats talk about agriculture as the sole source of wealth it is not agriculture in general that they have in mind, but capitalist agriculture" (Rubin 1979: 116, 124).

32 For an utterly contrasting reading, one that insists upon a notion of labor's intrinsic value, see Ernest Mandel's "Introduction" to Volume 1 of *Capital* (Mandel 1990 [1976]). In my estimation, Mandel completely fails to gauge properly the gap that marks the distance between Marx and the classical political economists. Mandel claims that the distinction between concrete

as it manifests in a social order structured by the logic of capital. Ryazanskaya's translation helps here, as he renders *spezifisch bürgerlich* as "a specifically bourgeois feature." This language has Marx (rightly, I would contend) suggesting to his readers that the very capacity for labor to produce exchange-value depends upon the structural dimensions of a social order centered on, and driven by, the logic of capital. In brief: only under capitalism can labor create exchange-value, because only capitalism creates the object Marx calls *exchange-value-positing-labor.*

This crucial historical contextualization effected by Marx's reading of Steuart simultaneously provides him with the background against which he will address the work of the most famous (to us) and most important (for Marx) political economists, Smith and Ricardo. Smith's answer to the question of how to understand the value of commodities appears squarely within the context of Steuart's establishment that exchange-value-producing-labor is not an ontological fact, but a definite historical construction of specific capitalist practices. And Smith's significance to political economy's development cannot be dissociated from his own conceptual slippages. Ironically, Smith's impact on the history of thought on capitalism (and value) is bound up with the fact that his own text lacks a clear thesis on the tripartite relation of value/commodities/labor, for the precise reason that it offers not one, but two, conflicting theses on the matter.[33]

---

labor and abstract labor "is a revolutionary step forward [by Marx] beyond Ricardo" (Mandel 1990: 42), when, in fact, that distinction can easily be found in Ricardo, who follows Smith directly on the idea of "labor in general." Marx himself points all this out, which explains why someone like Arthur can write succinctly "Mandel is *directly refuted* by Marx's own text" (Marx 1969a; Marx 1969b; cf. Marx 1996: 149; Arthur 2004: 55, emphasis added).

33 In this context, Mirowski makes a crucial argument, which is to claim that Smith's confusion about value and labor may be understood as a basic consequence of the fact that Smith's overriding theory of value *was not a labor theory*, but rather a stock theory. Here is Mirowski on Smith's *Wealth of Nations*: "by the time we reach Book 2, we discover *value is stock*, and that stock will be analyzed independent of relative price changes, a formless incompressible jelly, effortlessly rendered suitable for either consumption or investment. In a manner of speaking, Smith avoided the value conun-

Smith's major contribution to our understanding of capitalism, as Marx tells the story in numerous places, comes from his formalization of the inchoate understanding articulated by Franklin. Smith gives his readers, and future political economists, the concept of "labor in general" — an intellectual production that Marx elsewhere unequivocally names "an immense step forward" (Marx 1996: 149; see Chambers 2014: 98–105). Going back to Petty, Marx makes it clear that "labor in general" should be understood as "the entire *social aspect* of labor as it appears," particularly within the very division of labor that Smith unceasingly celebrates (Marx 2009: 24, emphasis added).

This means that *as Marx reads him,* Smith's "labor in general" is absolutely not "labor itself." Paradoxically, as Marx explains elsewhere, "labor in general" is a particular historical form of labor (Marx 1996: 151; Chambers 2014: 103). Labor in general (*Arbeit überhaupt*) is exchange-value-positing-labor (*Tauschwert setzende Arbeit*). I draw this conclusion here from my analysis of Marx's reading of the political economists, but the

---

drum that had so engrossed his predecessors by essentially bypassing it save for some early comments on labor, which are dropped in the subsequent analysis" (Mirowski 1989: 166–67). As I noted in an earlier footnote, Dobb also eschews the traditional reading of Smith as holding to a "labor theory of natural value" (Dobb 1973: 45). Dobb phrases the point with typical English understatement: "it cannot be said that Adam Smith made much use of this conception of a measure of value in terms of labour, in either of the senses to which he alludes" (Dobb 1973: 50). Thus, like Mirowski after him, Dobb downplays the idea of a contradiction between "labor-embodied" and "labor-commanded" and instead emphasizes the importance of capital stock and its "continual increase" (Dobb 1973: 49, 51, 52). Intentionally or not I cannot say, but Mirowksi's text presents Dobb's position utterly unfairly. Mirowski writes: "the quarrel over whether Smith confused labor-embodied and labor-commanded values (Dobb 1973) is, *for our purposes,* beside the point" (Mirowski 1989: 166, emphasis added). To spell things out: with his precise placement of the parenthetical citation, Mirowski's text *attributes to Dobb* a reiteration of emphasis on the putative confusion of labor-embodied with labor-commanded, while Mirowski deprecates the importance of this dispute so that he may then, uniquely, emphasize the idea, in Smith, of value as stock. However, as I have already shown, and as his text makes palpably clear, it was Dobb himself who first *resisted* the traditional reading of Smith and suggested the importance of value as stock.

statement comes directly from the opening of this very chapter in *Zur Kritik*: "exchange-value-positing-labor is *abstract
general* labor" ("Tauschwert setzende Arbeit ist daher abstrakt
allgemeine Arbeit") (Marx 2009: 7). This labor can be grasped
as "general" in contradistinction to concrete labor practices,
which are specific, but it is decisively not transhistorical — not
a philosophical essence, not a Platonic *eidos*. Labor in general
is not "labor itself" in a transcendental sense, because labor in
general only emerges within a capitalist social formation, only
first appears as a particular, historical type of labor, exchange-
value-producing-labor.

Smith, however, sees almost none of the above points. Having established the facticity of "labor in general" as if it were
a metaphysical truth (rather than a historical one), Smith then
equivocates, or confuses himself (the text is not determinative
here). Working in both cases with the idea of labor in general,
Smith makes two competing claims. On the one hand, he contends that the value of commodities is determined by the labor
(*sans phrase*) contained within them — i.e., the labor required
for their production. "What everything really costs to the man
who wants to acquire it, is the toil and trouble of acquiring it"
(Smith 1999 [1776]: 133).[34] On the other hand, he asserts that the

---

34 It is worth noting the degree of equivocation or tension even within this
single definition of value by Smith. Classical political economy is usually
taken to determine the value of commodities as the labor required to produce a commodity for the capitalist market, and Smith himself is seen to
support this thesis. But in this, perhaps the single clearest line in his text
in terms of articulating such a claim, Smith actually appears to refer to a
pre-capitalist sense of production. That is, "the toil and trouble of acquiring" something tends to evoke images of a Lockean state of nature, with its
Robinson Crusoe-like figures planting corn and picking apples. In such a
case, labor is *not* the Smithian labor *sans phrase* but rather the particular,
concrete labor of producing an object directly for its use-values. (That is,
we want the apple and the corn to eat them, not to trade them. On this
front, Ricardo surely "exceeds" Smith by suggesting that hunter-gatherers
produced for exchange.) In contrast, and as I describe in the text above,
Smith's general position is taken to refer to a capitalist process of production
where "labor" is the labor of producing a commodity for exchange. Smith's
text is riven by these sorts of conflations of pre-capitalist "acquisition" with

value of commodities can be understood in terms of the labor that they themselves can buy or control — that is, by the amount of labor one can exchange them for: "The value of any commodity, therefore, to the person who possesses it…is equal to the quantity of labour which it enables him to purchase or command" (Smith 1999: 133).

Yet Smith himself does not pose these as two alternatives. Rather — and as Marx sees it, much to his detriment — Smith seems to think that the two accounts are compatible (perhaps even that they are the same). Indeed, the two quotes I have given above to illustrate each of Smith's two respective articulations of the value of commodities appear back-to-back in Smith's own text. He presents them not as two distinct theses, but as different formulation of the same claim. Nonetheless, the two positions are neither the same nor equivalent. In his own exegesis of Smith here, Marx moves quite quickly (not giving the quotes I provide, above). More to the point, Marx does not even bother to detail what he surely thinks is obvious (and which he remarks on in greater detail in different contexts[35]): the amount of labor-time necessary to produce a commodity does not equal the value of that commodity when translated into a certain number of wage hours. For example, if it takes 4 labor-hours (so-called man-hours) to produce commodity A, and the going wage-rate is $5/hour, there is simply no reason to assume that the value/price of A will be $20. In fact, as other political economists (including, but by no means solely, Marx) show, there is every reason to believe that the price of the commodities will exceed $20. Furthermore, were that price not to exceed $20 this fact would itself

---

bourgeois production. Indeed, in a different context one could make the case that the powerful historical importance of Smith's text can be linked back to the (surely unintentional) productivity of these very conflations: Smith theorizes capitalism through a series of substitutions of Lockean individuals for capitalist workers, thereby naturalizing capitalism (cf. Smith 1999).

35 The Smithian contradiction (resolved but not overcome by Ricardo) centers Marx's analysis in the lecture he gave in 1865 ("Value, Price and Profit"), where it serves to construct the paradox that Marx's concept of "labor-power" sets out to resolve — or better, make manifest (Marx 1995: 13).

be taken as evidence of a firm on its way out of business — or perhaps as a sign of a temporarily dysfunctional market (one in which supply has by no means "equilibrated" demand).[36]

Marx condenses his entire presentation of Smith into a succinct formulation of the Smithian contradiction (between the two theses on the value of commodities in terms of labor), and then Marx suggests that the explanation for Smith's own confusion can be linked to Smith's failure to understand the "social aspect" of production under capitalism. Here is the key quote from Marx:

> Adam Smith constantly confuses the determination of the value of commodities by the labour-time contained in them with the determination of their value by the value of labour; ...he mistakes the objective equalisation of unequal quanti-

---

36 In *Capital*, Marx dismissively refutes the "vulgar" economists' view that the forces of supply and demand could serve as the source for an *increase* in value; he does so by asserting that exchange is always the exchange of equivalents and can therefore never be the source of value (Marx 1990: 260). However, these well-known passages are easily misread, in two different ways: first, by taking Marx to dismiss all of classical political economy (and replace it with his own economic theory); second, by taking Marx to dismiss the very idea that supply and demand are economic forces. With respect to the first, we can clarify by underscoring that Marx himself *distinguishes* between the "classical political economists" and the "vulgar economists." The former body of work, he argues throughout his career, is filled with important insights and discoveries, along with significant errors and confusions (which Marx proposes to criticize and overcome). The latter, however, make the mistake of taking the terms of classical political economy and thoroughly *naturalizing* them. In this sense, we might say that some of the classical economists have "vulgarizing" tendencies, but when Marx refers to the "vulgar" economists he explicitly does *not* mean Smith, Ricardo, Petty, Steuart, Say, etc. I elaborate on this point in my reading of Rubin in the following chapter. With respect to the latter misreading, one needs to emphasize that Marx well understood the existence and function of the forces of supply and demand. What he rejected — and here he *follows* Smith and Ricardo — was the idea that those forces could themselves *explain value*. Rather, as Marx spells out much more helpfully in the "Value, Price and Profit" lecture than he does in *Capital*, supply and demand can "explain to you why the market price of a commodity rises above or sinks below its *value*, but they can never account for *value* itself" (Marx 1995: 10–11).

ties of labour forcibly brought about by the social process for the subjective equality of the labours of individuals. (Marx 2009: 25)

In the first sentence Marx is merely pointing to the contradiction in Smith's two claims that I have unpacked above. The argument comes straight from Ricardo, who builds his project of political economy on a patient and detailed delineation of the Smithian inconsistency; much of Ricardo's greatest contribution to the field of political economy emerges out of his argument for why one of Smith's theses is valid, the other invalid (Ricardo 2001 [1821]: 9–10). Marx does more than claim that Smith is in contradiction with himself; having read Ricardo, Marx takes that point as obvious to any student of political economy.[37] Marx goes further, in that he explains what leads Smith into this impasse: Smith's confusion of the value of commodities with the value of labor *depends upon a logically prior confusion* of (A) the objective process by which a capitalist social formation "forcibly" renders "unequal quantities" of labor somehow *equal* to one another, and (B) the idea that distinct, concrete labors of individuals could somehow be the same, be "equal."

Any effort to grasp Marx's own understanding of value in relation to labor and capital depends on discerning how and why Marx sees (A) as not simply valid but essential to capitalism, and (B) as not simply wrong but deeply confused and mystifying with respect to our conceptual comprehension of a capitalist order. To elucidate Marx's position we need first to make some sense of his frustrating use and repetition of the word "equal." For Marx, we might say that capitalism is that social order that accomplishes the "equalisation" of distinct, "unequal" quantities of labor. "Equalisation" here refers to the process by which commodities can be equated to one another because they can be exchanged. Under capitalism, and only under capitalism,

---

37 Perhaps one reason Marx is hard for us to read today is that we likely have not read Ricardo (particularly not recently or thoroughly), yet Marx always assumes that we have.

three pairs of socks can be "equal to" two cans of soup. "Unequal quantities" therefore simply means different quantities, but the point — and the otherwise awkward way of putting the point; that is, the reason Marx says "unequal" rather than different — is a deeper one. We know that $3 \neq 2$, and yet we also know that, within the terms of a capitalist market, three pairs of socks = two cans of soup can be an utterly valid equation. This is just the sense in which Marx declares that the "objective equalisation of unequal quantities" is the profound result of capitalism. As the quote from above indicates, the process is both *objective* and *social*, and it depends on *force*. This already demonstrates that there is nothing in the nature of commodities themselves that would inherently or inexorably lead to this process. And this is just why Marx, at the same time as he affirms part of Smith's analysis — part (A) — remains adamant, contra Smith, that the labor of the shoemaker and the labor of the carpenter are not the same. In the sense that they produce utterly different use-values, they could never be equal, since making a shoe and building a house are not the same activities (and neither are needing shoes and needing shelter the same needs).

Why does Smith make such an obvious, rudimentary mistake? This question seems crucially important, yet Ricardo never poses it. Neither does Marx, despite the fact that Marx's own analysis makes an answer to the question possible. Of course, there could be numerous hypothetical explanations, but I want to work though the most viable candidate for a response by building from my reading of Marx. From that perspective, Smith contradicts himself due to his own failure to conceptualize labor in general as the particular type of labor (exchange-value-positing-labor) that it is and must be. In other words, Smith often implies that labor in general simply *is* labor itself (a generic and transhistorical force); if this were so, then the general labor required to produce a commodity and the general labor such a commodity commands would necessarily be equal. The equation would be validated not by the economic arithmetic but by metaphysical definitions. Marx contributes to the explanation as follows: "[Smith] tries to accomplish the transition from concrete labour to exchange-value-positing-labor, i.e., the basic form of bourgeois labour, by means of the division of labour" (Marx 2009: 25, translation modified). Smith repeatedly calls on the division of labor as a sort of *magical force*. These are my words, but I do not use them casually or hyperbolically: Smith's own text gives the reader this sense of the inherent, overwhelming power of the division of labor. Here Marx is suggesting that Smith desires a division of labor that serves as an elementary particle, a fundamental force, to effect the transition from distinct concrete labors (the shoemaker and the carpenter) to labor *sans phrase,* which as Marx has shown is precisely exchange-value-setting-labor. But because Smith cannot see that labor in general is not labor itself, that *Arbeit überhaupt* can never be anything other than *Tauschwert setzende Arbeit,* he thus goes on to ascribe the same sort of transhistorical force to the division of labor that he thinks resides within labor in general.

Despite its central importance to his overall account, Marx's critical reply to Smith may appear elliptical to some readers. My conceptual and exegetical work above throws Marx's criticism into sharper relief: "But though it is correct to say that individual exchange presupposes division of labour, it is wrong to maintain that division of labour presupposes individual exchange" (Marx 2009: 25). This very specific critique of Smith will eventually become a general claim in the first chapter of the first volume of *Capital* (Marx 1990: 132). In both cases, Marx contends that in order to have capitalist exchange of commodities, one must already have a developed division of labor; one cannot conceive of producing objects for their inherent exchange-value — making them only in order to sell them — without assuming a division of labor, and this is because exchange-value is never "inherent," but always *social.* However, the reverse is not at all true. Without breaking any rules of logic, we can easily imagine a social order with a highly advanced division of labor, one wherein goods are produced (even traded) directly for their use-values (or perhaps on some other basis entirely). Each labor, though divided from other labors, would be a distinct, concrete labor, not an element of labor in general. The labor of workers would be specific to their trade, because exchange-value-positing-labor would not exist. To concretize the point, Marx offers the historical example of the Peruvians: a society with a highly developed division of labor, but no capitalist exchange (Marx 2009: 25).[38] In other words, one can only have exchange-value-positing-labor against a background of a given division of labor, but the division of labor does not itself give rise to exchange-value-producing-labor. Smith's mistake is that he thinks the "labor in general" developed by bourgeois society is nothing other than a "labor itself" as it has appeared throughout time and across all space.

As Marx reads him, Ricardo overcomes Smith's error, yet then manages to repeat it in even more egregious form. Ricardo exceeds Smith in his clear articulation of the historical preconditions required for the emergence of exchange-value-positing-labor. Here Marx uses a slightly different phrase, one that proves crucial to grasping his overall account of value. Following a quote from Ricardo concerning the emergence of capitalist industry and competition, Marx writes: "the full development of the law of value (*Gesetz des Wertes*) presupposes a society in which large-scale industrial production and free competition obtain, in other words modern bourgeois society" (Marx 2009: 25). Alas, despite this apparent insight, Ricardo spends much of his time projecting all of the features of "modern bourgeois" society back onto historical or mythical times and places. Marx cannot help but ridicule Ricardo for the profound depth of the latter's anachronistic thinking:

> Ricardo's primitive fisherman and primitive hunter are from the outset owners of commodities who exchange their fish and game in proportion to the labour-time which is mate-

---

38 Marx also clarifies what he means in the quote above by "individual exchange"—namely, "exchange of products in the form of commodities" (Marx 2009: 25). Elsewhere Marx emphasizes the extent to which the "individuated individual" is itself the product of a capitalist social order, an argument that undoes and utterly reverses a liberal account of society whereby autonomous individuals construct a society through their consent (Marx 1996: 129).

rialised in these exchange-values. On this occasion he slips into the anachronism of allowing the primitive fisherman and hunter to calculate the value of their implements in accordance with the annuity tables used on the London Stock Exchange in 1817. (Marx 2009: 25).

Thus we might say, in the language I have been developing here, that Ricardo's analysis contains the evidence needed to demonstrate the distinction — the very difference Smith continuously elides — between, on the one hand, labor in general as the form of appearance of exchange-value-positing-labor and, on the other, the transhistorical "labor itself" *hypostatized* by Smith. Yet Ricardo himself fails to grasp the implications of that evidence, and thereby winds up with even worse hypostatizations than Smith before him.[39]

* * *

And yet, Marx's merciless mockery of Ricardo should not be mistaken for dismissal. He closes out his genealogy by stressing that even though he is "encompassed by this bourgeois horizon, Ricardo *analyses* bourgeois economy [with] theoretical acumen" (Marx 2009: 25, emphasis added). Perhaps a genealogist can pay no higher compliment: as I noted earlier, in order to do a history of the present, one must have the capacity to *think* the social order of which one is a part — so much so as to render that present *alien*. Marx homes in on just this point, giving his final line to one of Ricardo's contemporaries, who said of him: "Mr. Ricardo seemed as if he had dropped from another planet" (Marx 2009: 25, quoting Lord Brougham). All of which explains

---

39 Marx's text ends with a mention of Sismondi, but this seems a mere footnote given that, in terms of the logical force of Marx's argument, Ricardo surely serves as the end point of Marx's genealogical analysis. Hence Marx's most important claim about Sismondi may well be this dismissive remark: "Whereas Ricardo's political economy ruthlessly draws its final conclusion and therewith ends, Sismondi supplements this ending by expressing doubt in political economy itself" (Marx 2009: 25).

Marx's praise of Ricardo as the thinker who "gave to political economy its final shape"; for Marx, the animating arguments of classical political economy amount to critical engagements with and against Ricardo (Marx 2009: 26; cf. Sraffa 1951).[40]

This brings us to one of the strongest pieces of evidence in favor of reading Marx as a genealogist: although his archeology of classical political economy goes forward rather than backward in time, it still ends neither with *telos* nor with *Ursprung*, but strictly with what Foucault helpfully calls "the space of a dispersion" (Foucault 1972: 10). This is precisely what Marx's genealogy of value within classical political economy produces: a space of dispersion, both in the sense of a clearing, an opening for new work, and in terms of a fracturing, an undoing of the classical political economists' account of value through Marx's incessant critique. Marx's own account of value and the value-form can thus be understood in terms provided by Foucault, as a *deployment* of that very space of dispersion.

---

40 And Marx is clear that the majority of thinkers in the nineteenth century fail to measure up to, or even understand the arguments of Ricardo. From the perspective developed here (that of a genealogical Marx) we might say that the genius of Ricardo is to have grasped value relations under capitalism, to understand "relative value" (Sraffa 1951: xxxvi). Despite this, and as Sraffa illuminates, Ricardo never abandoned, but surely also never reached, the ultimate goal of locating an "invariable measure" of "absolute value" (Sraffa 1951: xlvi). Marx has been consistently misinterpreted over the years by readers who fail to see how often Marx's scathing polemical critiques of specific authors (particularly the socialist utopians) can often be boiled down to Marx yelling at the author in question, "you idiot, have you not read your Ricardo?" The misreading results from mistaking Marx's arguments for Ricardo's by taking such passages as evidence of Marx holding a particular position, rather than his merely pointing at Ricardo's arguments as a decisive refutation of whatever the author in question has claimed.

CHAPTER THREE

Value and the Value-Form in a Capitalist Social Formation_

LTV and VFT_

Where does Marx's genealogical reading of the classical political economists leave us with respect to the general question of the relation between labor and value under capitalism? That is, where has Marx's genealogy *taken us*? And in particular, what perspective does Marx's encounter with political economy afford us on our own efforts to understand value within (neoliberal) capitalism? What can we see better or differently at the end of this journey?

We might first take stock of Marx's overall reading. He wishes to affirm the idea that a bourgeois social formation produces a new, unique type of labor: exchange-value-positing-labor. More importantly, the type of labor that can itself "produce" or "set" exchange-value is absolutely not any sort of particular, concrete form of labor; neither sewing clothes, nor mining gold ore, nor any other specific form of labor can be understood as exchange-value-positing-labor. Only labor in general (*Arbeit überhaupt*) is exchange-value-setting-labor (*Tauschwert setzende Arbeit*). Perhaps most significantly, "labor in general" is itself a highly developed form of labor — one that emerges exclusively under a capitalist social order, but only where there develops a certain *indifference* to the type of labor done, since all labor is labor for the production of commodities (exchange-values) and all labor is wage-labor (Marx 1996: 150; see Murray 1999a: 45). But this set of facts entails something crucially important for Marx: labor in general, a monumental developmental achievement of capitalism, is not, and can never be conflated with, *labor itself*. Smith's error, reprised by Ricardo, is the failure to see the difference between, on the one hand, a generalized abstract labor that takes shape *within* capitalism and, on the other, a generic idea of a transhistorical labor — an idea of labor as an essential metaphysical force for all times and places.

It is in this context, and only now, here at the end of the genealogical journey, that we might productively turn our attention to the so-called *labor theory of value* (LTV). The labor theory of value is a textbook answer to the question, as I summarized it at the beginning of the previous chapter, "where does value come from?" According to the LTV, value comes from labor, which has an intrinsic, essential — indeed, universal — power to bestow value on the objects it produces. The innate source of the value *in* commodities is thus the labor required to create those commodities in the first place; value in society can be traced directly to labor as its locus. The LTV provides a straightforward, concise, and sharp account of value in relation to capitalist commodities, and it generalizes this account to an understanding of value across all time and place. Moreover, from Marx's genealogical reading of the political economists, we can witness numerous ways in which *those thinkers* might be seen to articulate, support, or subscribe to the LTV. Smith, in particular, sees "labor itself" as the fount of value, and he thereby offers a general, metaphysical account of value — both under capitalism and elsewhere.[1]

---

1   As I mentioned in a previous chapter note, Mirowski's work provides a powerful wide-angle lens for viewing the entire history of modern, western economic thought in terms of the question of value. For him, the paradigm for classical political economy (*including Marx*) was a *substance* theory of value, while the marginalist revolution that marks the neoclassical para-

Marx's genealogy of the political economists thus makes it starkly, unquestionably clear that he himself does not endorse, support, or in any way subscribe to *this classical version of* LTV (see Arthur 2004: 55).[2] At its core, the LTV rests on an idea of "labor itself," the very concept that Marx takes Smith (and Ricardo) to task for endorsing. Marx's insistence on the contrast between "labor in general" and "labor itself," his account of exchange-value-setting-labor as the *historical achievement* of capitalism, and his refusal of the idea that different concrete labors (weaving and painting, for example) could be "equalized" — all of this amounts to a thoroughgoing rejection of the LTV. Indeed, Marx's genealogy of classical political economy gives us the perspective needed to see the LTV as a rather strange idea. For Marx, labor has no intrinsic, metaphysical powers that would allow it

---

digm depends on a field theory of value — based on a proto-energetics metaphor borrowed from mid-nineteenth-century Physics (Mirowski 1989). In a certain sense, I concur with everything Mirowski says about the general program of classical political economy; from my perspective, Mirowski just fails to see that Marx, too, was *analyzing* this paradigm (not merely working within it) and was thus offering his own *critique* of it. In doing so — that is, in providing his analysis of the value-form — Marx produced an alternative to *both* the classical and the neoclassical value paradigms. This also explains the frequency with which critiques of neoclassicism either actively invoke a substantialist account of value (e.g., Sraffa 1960; Keynes 1964) or are simply assumed to be doing so.

2 This is not, of course, to say that Marx does not develop his own account of how value is established within a capitalist social formation *in relation to labor*. Thus, we might well say that Marx has a theory of value that is related to labor, and some might want to go further to describe this as *Marx's own version of the* LTV. Logically such a move is surely tenable, but for at least two reasons I choose not to make it. First, there is a long history of referring to Marx's version of the LTV as precisely the same as the classical LTV, so the reference to "Marx's LTV" would easily be misunderstood for the very theory that Marx himself rejected. Second, the phrase "labor theory of value" connotes something quite different than genealogy and is therefore misleading from the outset; LTV suggests the sort of metaphysical account whereby essential properties of things produce definite effects. As the previous chapter has shown, Marx produces a historical account, a genealogy of value under the specific and concrete terms of a capitalist social formation, and in this sense he has no general "theory," whether it be the LTV or anything else (see Chambers 2017).

to "create value." The classical political economists saw labor as the source of value, in the sense of an *Ursprung*, a metaphysical origin. Marx saw it differently, because his genealogy refused the concept of an *Ursprung* to begin with; he rejected the idea of what I would call an "elementary particle" — something that could stand outside the social formation and explain its development.[3] These central and significant differences make Marx's critique an entire displacement of the paradigm of classical political economy, a whole new way to understand value in a social order itself — not some minor quibbling over the particular way the classical political economists conceived of value. The creation of value under capitalism is always, for Marx, a systemic effect of a capitalist social order.[4]

---

3 It is often thought that Marx identifies just such an elementary particle in his frequent references to "labor-power," and it would be easy enough to take "labor-power" as a physical force in nature, one that creates value. But especially in his later works, when Marx refers to "labor-power" he is not referring to the general "power of labor." For Marx, "labor-power" is an absolutely specialized term (arguably the most important such term in all of *Capital*), since it names/describes the unique historico-political creation of the very commodity that is essential to capitalism. "Labor-power," says Marx, is not a force, but a thing. It is a commodity — and not just any commodity, but a unique commodity. Capitalists can use their access to large-scale means of production to produce commodities for exchange and sell them. During the transition to capitalism, small-crafts producers, calling on access to small scale means of production, can also create commodities and sell them. But after the transition to developed capitalism, we have the emergence of an entire class of people with no capital, and no access to means of production. They have no objective commodities to sell. Their only choice, then, is to work for a wage, an act that Marx re-describes — under the specific terms of capitalism in which everything is subject to market exchange — as a worker selling his "labor-power." Labor-power is the only commodity you have when you have no commodities at all. But this makes labor-power a specific product of capitalist historical development. It could not be further from a transhistorical force (cf. Rubin 2008: 24).

4 Marx's historico-epistemological feat: he establishes an "elementary particle" (the entity that performs the social function of having/bestowing intrinsic value) that is itself historically produced. Thus, while the classical political economists do indeed see labor as the source of intrinsic value in a capitalist political economy, Marx does not agree with them. The genealogy from the previous chapter reveals Marx hard at work trying to prove

But the question of how to understand value under capitalism cannot be reduced to an either/or choice vis-a-vis the LTV. There are good reasons why Marx has so often, and so consistently, been *misread* as somehow articulating his own version of the LTV; let me identify two. The first has been succinctly summarized by Paul Mason, who shows how the history of Marxism as a political movement on behalf of the working class helps to explain why Marx would be mistaken for an LTV theorist — in particular, because working class radical politics derived so much leverage and inspiration from a *Ricardian LTV*. Mason captures the historical turn as follows: "after Ricardo, the labour-theory [of value] became the signature idea of industrial capitalism," being used to "justify profits" and "attack the landed aristocracy." But it soon thereafter "proved subversive. It created an argument for who gets what, which the factory owners immediately started to lose. Amid the candlelight of the pubs where the early trade unions met, David Ricardo suddenly had a whole new set of followers" (Mason 2015: 149). Yet one cannot hesitate to add: it is precisely what Mason calls the "doctrine of 'Ricardian socialism'" that Marx himself is at such pains to re-

---

inadequate the answers given by classical political economy. Keen observation of the development of bourgeois society shows that there is no such thing as labor itself. Rather, while capitalism does establish "labor in general" (something that had not existed before capitalism, since concrete labors were always different when one was producing use-values directly), *labor in general is not labor itself.* The labor in general achieved by capitalist development is itself a definite, very specific type of labor — namely, exchange-value-positing-labor. Marx therefore does have an answer to the question, "what is the source of value under capitalism?" It is exchange-value-positing-labor. Yet Marx's answer, while apparently similar both to that given by classical political economy, and to the terms of the static and generalized "labor theory of value" turns out, in fact, to be a radical, and utterly revolutionary departure from that theory. As I make clear in the text, I am not the first to say any of this. The surprise is not to learn that Marx rejects the LTV, but that so many of Marx's readers have failed to notice. In the text I try to avoid becoming mired in those old debates — partially because the value-form theorists have already won, but mainly because I have a different purpose here. I focus on Marx's ability to show that what I am calling the "elementary particle" cannot stand outside the system but is rather a product of that system.

fute in his frequent attacks on socialist utopianism (Marx 1995b; Marx 1996).

Moving from history to, second, the terms of theory, I want to look more closely at Marx's understanding of "the law of value" that he points to in his reading of Ricardo; I do so in order to analyze how that "law" relates to Marx's broader understanding of the "form of value" under capitalism. To put the point in condensed form: *Marx is mistaken for an* LTV *theorist precisely because his goal is not merely to refute the* LTV, *but to show how something like the* LTV *could emerge within capitalism in the first place.* To unpack this formulation requires stepping back from the particulars of Marx's reading of the classical political economists to take a wider view of his understanding of value and the value-form (*Wertform*). Here I turn to a long and rich, yet still surprisingly neglected, tradition of interpreting Marx in terms of the form of value.

The histories of various schools of interpretation of Marx, not to mention Marxism, prove multiply fractured and highly complex. I will not provide a contextualist reconstruction of all those histories. However, I think it safe to say that today we can trace the tradition of the value-form reading of Marx, or "value-form theory" (VFT), to the early work and lasting influence of Hans-Georg Backhaus, a student of Adorno whose 1965 seminar work is now seen as the source-point for what would later become VFT, also known as *Neue Marx-Lektüre* (NML).[5]

---

5   The phrase *neue Marx-Lektüre* was first used by Backhaus himself in the preface to a collection of his essays (Backhaus 1997; see Heinrich 2012: 229n2). While, to repeat, there are no self-identified or consciously practicing schools here, we can say that NML and VFT are roughly "the same" because the "New Reading of Marx" is a reading that hinges on re-emphasizing Marx's understanding of the form of value. Often the general gloss for NML is that it departs from scientific or deterministic accounts of Marx in order to return to his critique of political economy and connect that project to his larger critique (or understanding) of society. To show how Marx does this, thinkers within the NML tradition attend closely to Marx's understanding of the value-form. Hence, in many ways, NML names the broad approach to Marx, and VFT names the substantive hinge. Both VFT and NML can be distinguished from, but also overlap with, *Wertkritik*, an approach devel-

Since the development of the NML, many well-known and well-respected figures have continued to read and to criticize Marx as either subscribing to the LTV, endorsing his own version of it, or otherwise seeing value as an "objective" or "physiological" property of commodities (Wolff 1981; Keen 1993a; Carver 1998). But the conclusions I have drawn above — that Marx absolutely departs from an LTV, that his task is not to modify that theory but to explain its very emergence — would come as no surprise whatsoever to value-form theorists. Indeed, the central point of departure for a VFT reading of Marx lies in rethinking the very question of value and capitalism. Here is how Bellofiore and Riva put it in their recent introduction and overview of NML:

> What actually distinguishes Marx's critique of political economy from the economic theories before him, as well as those after him, is the theory of the *form* of value. Marx's critique of political economy tries to answer the following questions. Why value? Why is value nothing but an expression of labour? What are the conditions of possibility of the existence of value, which is an "objective social dimension," according to which commodities are exchanged? …These questions, which can be found more or less explicitly in *Capital* and in the preparatory works for *Capital* (at least from the *Grundrisse*), were, with very

---

oping somewhat later than (we now date) VFT, associated closely with the writings of Robert Kurz, focusing more on questions of reification or crisis, and more tightly linked to early forms of Frankfurt School Critical Theory. Backhaus's original seminar paper was translated and introduced more than a decade later by *Thesis Eleven* (see Eldred and Roth 1980; Backhaus 1980). For a very recent and helpful overview of NML, see Bellofiore and Riva 2015. For a recent text introducing *Wertkritik* to an English-speaking audience, see Larsen et al. 2014. My own work in the text below, concerning the emergence of VFT, focuses on Backhaus, but it needs to be said that he never worked in isolation: his original work was done under the supervision of Adorno, and a great deal of his output was completed in collaboration with Helmut Reichelt. I spend some time on a description of VFT and its history in order to situate my reading of Marx, and in this context I also want to mention other political theorists who have recently acknowledged the significance of VFT (Vatter 2014: chap. 2; Roberts 2017).

few exceptions, not seriously addressed by Marx's followers and interpreters. (Bellofiore and Riva 2015: 24)

From this perspective we can see that Marx does not try to
show *that* labor is the source of value, but rather to ask *why* that
should be so within a capitalist social formation.

Patrick Murray helpfully formulates the point by referring
to "Marx's idea that value comes not from labour but from a
historically specific form of labour" (Murray 1999: 34). In some
ways this formulation seems like nothing more than a matter
of emphasis, reflected in Murray's own use of italics, but a great
deal more is at stake. Werner Bonefeld, Richard Gunn, and Kosmas Psychopedis make a crucial contribution by distinguishing two understandings of form. On the one hand, we have an
analytic understanding of form as species, such that "the forms
of something are the specific character it can assume." On the
other hand, "'form' can be understood as a *mode of existence*:
something or other exists only in and through the form(s) it
takes" (Bonefeld, Gunn, and Psychopedis 1992: xv; see also Arthur 1979: 72). Applied to our example above, we can now see
how radical Murray's claim appears, and why it would make
sense to italicize "historically specific form" of labor. Murray is
suggesting not that labor is something transhistorical that takes
on different forms (form as species) at different moments in
time, but rather that there is a form of labor under capitalism,
and it is historically unique (form as mode of existence).

This type of work can all be traced back to Backhaus's early article, "On the Dialectics of the Value-Form," which itself
makes a powerful case for the *subtlety* of Marx's account of value
in terms of the value-form. Backhaus strongly suggests that part
of the difficulty in grasping Marx's conception of the value-
form — the aspect of his argument that Marx himself always
maintained was the most difficult to understand — was that
Marx, in effect, "dumbed down" his presentation as he repeat-

edly revised it (Marx 1990: 90; Backhaus 1980: 100).[6] Indirectly, then, Backhaus points readers of Marx back to the text that I took as my central focus in the previous chapter: according to Backhaus, *Zur Kritik* contains the first developed presentation of Marx's value-form analysis, and, I would add, perhaps the one that most maintains the dynamic, dialectical element that is essential to understanding Marx's sense of the historical development of a capitalist social formation.[7] Backhaus cites *Zur Kritik* extensively in order to advance his own account of the value-form.[8] Moreover, as I have shown in the previous chapter, the focus on *Zur Kritik* is no accident, since it is there that Marx emerges most clearly as genealogist.

My project is not a historical reconstruction of VFT, nor do I want to get lost in Marxological intricacies. Instead, I turn to VFT to demonstrate that my own engagement with Marx follows in the footsteps of relatively recent, but already rich tradition of

---

6   "Dumbed down" are my words, not Backhaus's, but they effectively capture a line of argument that Backhaus has consistently advanced over the years, starting with his original rhetorical question, "has Marx gone so far in his popularisation" in the opening sections of Volume 1 of *Capital* that the value-form can no longer be grasped (Backhaus 1980: 100; see Reichelt 1995, cited in Bonefeld 1998)?

7   This move may not be as radical as it seems, since Marx himself points the way to it in his preface to the first German edition of *Capital*. There Marx both emphasizes the importance of the value-form — saying "the human mind has sought in vain for more than 2,000 years to get to the bottom of it" — and admits that the presentation of the value-form in *Capital* is a "popularized" version of the fuller account in *Zur Kritik* (Marx 1990: 90).

8   Here may be the most opportune moment to emphasize that the value-form approach to Marx is best understood as an overall understanding of Marx's project — not, that is, a specific thread of his project that can be found only in a few key works. Therefore, while I focus on *Zur Kritik* — and while value-form theorists have often emphasized the first, German edition of volume 1 of *Capital* — I am not confining my arguments to any specific texts. Indeed, once one makes sense of what Marx means by the value-form, *Capital* and other more famous texts read quite differently. In short, Marx does not change his mind; he changes his formulation and presentation in a way that makes it easier to misread him on value. Backhaus points in just this direction, and other VFT and NML thinkers have done the work to prove these claims. I aim to demonstrate the salience of a VFT approach to Marx, not just for his texts, but for our contemporary understanding of capitalism.

reading Marx. My claims about the relationship between value and labor under capitalism are not necessarily all that new, even if they do fly in the face of still-canonized understandings of Marx as a critic of alienation and a celebrant of labor as the essential creator/producer of value.[9] Even the "New Marx Reading" is not *de novo*, since so much of the framework of the VFT approach to Marx is contained in a much earlier text, Isaak Illich Rubin's monumental interpretation of Marx, *Essays on Marx's Theory of Value* (2008 [1928]).[10] This work was long forgotten in the history of Marx scholarship and in the history of Marxism. And, significantly, Rubin remains uncited in Backhaus's seminal article, despite the fact that so much of what Backhaus calls for in the late 1960s was already provided by Rubin almost half a century before. Perhaps more importantly, in some ways Rubin is still forgotten: Bellofiore and Riva's overview of NML contains a rich, thorough, and very valuable set of citations, but they trace the development of NML only from the 1960s onward — hence Rubin goes unmentioned.

All of this means that new readers coming to this literature in the twenty-first century must grapple with, at the least, some cognitive dissonance, if not intellectual whiplash. On the one hand, and as shown above, a new reader encounters numerous (recent) works within the NML/VFT tradition that do not cite Rubin at all. On the other hand, one runs into claims like the following from Chris Arthur: "the most important single influence on the value-form approach to *Capital* was the rediscovery of

---

9   In emphasizing this continuity, and in pointing my work toward the rich body of VFT writings, I take a different tack than some. To take one prominent example, Moishe Postone's (1993) monumental work on Marx overlaps at numerous places with the work of VFT, but rather than trace these connections (or even acknowledge the debt), Postone spends a large proportion of his time working out and defining a "traditional Marxism" which serves as a foil meant to make Postone's work stand out as unique.

10   The first edition of Rubin's book was published in Russian in 1923. I am working with an English translation of the 1928 third edition (Rubin 2008), which is widely available on *marxists.org*. My references are to an Internet Archive version with static page numbers: https://archive.org/details/RubinEssaysOnMarxsTheoryOfValueClean.

the masterly exegesis of Marx's value theory by I. I. Rubin" (Arthur 2004: 11). It would be easy to quibble with Arthur's claim here, as formulated, since in my own reading of the value-form literature, it is simply not true that Rubin plays a central role. As I mentioned above, in Backhaus's seminal article Rubin goes unmentioned and he is not alone: many contributors to NML/ VFT do not discuss or even cite Rubin.[11] So if Arthur means to claim direct authorial influence — to suggest that VFT developed under the guidance of Rubin's interpretation — then I am not sure that the claim can hold up. But I prefer to read Arthur more charitably by interpreting him broadly, and thereby taking the "influence" claim somewhat metaphorically. That is to say, to read Rubin today, *after* VFT, is to see crisply and palpably how much Rubin's work anticipates, and in some ways still exceeds the writings of NML thinkers. For me, the power of Rubin's book is that it is *not* trapped in late twentieth-century debates about how to "get Marx right"; such debates often bogged down in semantic quarrels over "science" and "dialectics" — not to mention "systematic dialectics" versus "diamat," etc.[12] Hence, to a great extent I concur with Arthur because I think that it is hard to overstate the brilliance of Rubin's interpretation of value (and of Marx). If forced to recommend just one "secondary source" on Marx, I would choose Rubin's book.[13]

---

11 Murray, a member of what I am tempted to call the "American offshoot" of VFT (see Moseley 1993; Moseley and Campbell 1997; Moseley 2005) does engage substantively with Rubin (Murray 1999). But even Murray's treatment of Rubin is narrow: he takes up a very specific strand of Rubin's argument and develops a subtle response (subtle, because Murray wants to reach the same end as Rubin but through different, more sophisticated conceptual means). What my own survey of the VFT literature has never turned up is a broad, detailed reading of, and extensive engagement with, Rubin. In other words, I have not found the text that would serve as direct evidence for Arthur's claim of Rubin's *influence* on VFT.

12 For a rigorous and astute treatment of the question of dialectics, written through the lens of value-form theory, see Reuten 2000.

13 Although in many ways it would be unfair to call Rubin's book a secondary text, since it is not just a reading a Marx, but a broad and systematic presentation of its own. In other words, Rubin's project is designed primarily to

But more significant than how we situate or rank Rubin's work, his reading of Marx matters most because it helps us to rethink value under capitalism *today* — that is, under the terms of contemporary neoliberal capitalism. I turn to Rubin in order to connect my interpretation of Marx's genealogy of classical political economy with the larger question of value under investigation throughout my project.

Rethinking Fetishism_

Before considering Rubin's treatment of "Marx's theory of commodity fetishism" (Rubin 2008: 8), it is worth mapping out the wide gap between the meaning of "fetish" at the time of Marx's writing and today. This entails, first of all, underscoring the crucial origin of the term: it first appears within the context of early merchant capitalism. As David McNally nicely explains, European traders and colonizers invented the term as a way to explain *failures of the market*. Portuguese traders were befuddled and troubled by the fact that their African trading partners (or colonized subjects) simply refused to trade certain items (McNally 2011: 201–2). To explain such "irrational" behavior, they coined the term *feitiço*, a noun form of the adjective meaning "artificial," itself derived from the Latin *facticius*, meaning "made by art, artificial" (Harper 2016). A *feitiço* was a strange, utterly artificial, human valuation of an object that distorted its natural, market valuation, such that African traders refused to give up these *feitiço* objects, even when offered large sums of gold. The invention of the concept of a "fetish" killed two birds with one stone: "European merchants simultaneously construed their own marketised value relations as part of the natural order of things, while positing African customs and practices as outrageous violations of all that is decent and proper" (McNally 2011: 202). This idea of the fetish was then widely disseminated by Willem Bosman, whose book, *A New and Accurate Account*

---

understand value (under capitalism); defending and interpreting Marx are ancillary features of the work.

of the Guinea Coast, was first published in Dutch in 1703. Bosman's book was quickly translated into English, French, and German (all by 1706); Newton and Locke owned the book, and Adam Smith cites it (McNally 2011: 202).

But it was Charles de Brosses, in his *Du culte des dieux fétiches* (1760), who popularized the term precisely by literalizing, generalizing, and simplifying the idea of a fetish. De Brosses ruled out an allegorical reading of fetish and drove home the idea of the worship of idols. He thereby shifted the idea of a "fetish" from an "artificial" entity to an animated spiritual force, tying up the idea of fetish with religion and especially associating *fetishism* — a name for these religious practices of worshipping objects — with primitivism, ignorance, and backwardness (McNally 2011: 202). Marx first encounters the concept of the fetish early in his career when he reads a translation of de Brosses's work sometime in the late 1830s or early 1840s. This has led many a reader of Marx to assume that the concept of "fetish" that Marx uses simply is that of de Brosses's. However, building on the monumental work of William Pietz, Richard Boer helpfully shows that Marx put the idea of the fetish into his toolkit early on, and "even he could perhaps not foresee quite what would become of the idea" within his own work (Boer 2010: 97).

Synthesizing and extrapolating, let me now draw out four crucial points:

1. The problem/concept/idea of "fetish" emerges within the context of early merchant capitalism and colonialism; it is by no means merely a separate anthropological concept that is then translated or applied to "economics."
2. "Fetish" and "fetishism," while undoubtedly closely related, cannot be conflated without significant implications. The analysis of an object as a "fetish" object is simply not the same thing as the delineation of a set of rituals or practices as "fetishism." Marx himself usually refers not to the fetishism of commodities, but to the commodity's fetish-character (cf. Schulz 2012).

3. Perhaps it should go without saying, but just to be on the safe side: the entire history of *sexual* fetishism post-dates Marx entirely. There is scholarly debate over exactly when the idea of a sexual fetish is first introduced, with 1887 and 1897 as the most likely candidates. Both of those dates, however, come after Marx's writings, and the broader general idea of *fetishizing* something in the sense of fixating on it as an object of desire (whether it be an elbow or a sports car) comes later.

4. The fact that Marx gets the idea of the "fetish" from his reading of de Brosses cannot serve as evidence that he uses the concept the way de Brosses does. Indeed, as we will see, the evidence indicates quite the contrary.

With this context in mind, we can now turn to Rubin. To today's readers, Rubin's title, *Essays on Value*, might suggest a narrow focus for the book, but this would be wholly misleading. Rubin offers, above all, a hermeneutic approach — more *a way of reading* Marx than a specific interpretation. And this hermeneutics cuts directly against the grain not only of twentieth-century Marxisms, but also of modern economics. Both the start and end point of Rubin's approach centers on "fetishism";[14] his primary move consists in refusing the idea that fetishism is but a supplementary feature of Marx's argument in *Capital*. Rubin resists even the idea that "fetishism" is a separate step or element in Marx's broader argument, which makes the reading so radical as to *appear* to deny an obvious fact — since Marx's discussion of the fetish occurs in its own separately numbered and titled section of chapter 1 of Volume 1 of *Capital*.[15] Rubin places

---

14 The English translation of Rubin's Russian thereby loses the distinction that I would otherwise want to maintain between "fetish character" and "fetishism." Nonetheless, Rubin's broader analysis supports and complements an emphasis on the idea of the fetish character of the commodity.

15 Today we can easily amass much evidence to indicate that the presentation of fetishism as supplemental is both an artifact of the editorial and publishing history of the later volumes of *Capital* and in many ways, as Backhaus suggests, a distortion of Marx's original ideas (Backhaus 1980: 102). Prior to the publication of the first German edition of Volume 1, Marx — at Engels's urging — reworked earlier drafts of the first chapter of *Capital* so as

his radical thesis just where introductory English composition courses say it should go (at the end of the first paragraph): "the theory of fetishism is, *per se*, the basis of Marx's entire economic system, and in particular of his theory of value" (Rubin 2008: 8).

To uphold such a strong claim, Rubin first has to show that "commodity fetishism" is not something ancillary or additional (something that may or may not happen to, or in relation with, commodities), but rather, that fetishism proves to be so primary that "commodity fetishism" becomes, in a way, redundant. He then has to demonstrate that Marx's broad conceptualization of the social order and his particular understanding of value both follow and operationalize the logic of the fetish. Rubin sets out to overturn an entire history of "generally accepted views" concerning Marx and fetishism. In doing so, I would suggest, Rubin cuts against the grain of the standard view of Marx's understanding of fetishism that will continue to be propounded throughout the twentieth and into the twenty-first century. Rubin succinctly summarizes the standard view whereby "fetishism" indicates that relations between things (commodities) mask or hide relations among people, and in this way the "theory of fetishism" proves to be "critical" in the sense of *demystifying*: it unmasks illusions, showing that commodity relations are only superficial

---

to simplify the presentation. Yet Marx still very much wanted to mark the importance of "the value-form," and therefore in the first German edition he included an appendix with that very title. In this appendix, Marx stressed that any commodity had a "natural form," a "tangible, sensible form of existence," and also a "social form," the "value-form." Marx goes on to lay out the "peculiarities" of the equivalent form of commodities, but unlike later editions of *Capital* in which we find three peculiarities, Marx, in the appendix to the first German edition, includes a fourth, "the fetishism of the commodity-form" (Marx 1978 [1867]). Backhaus hence makes the obvious, but no less significant, claim that "theory of the fetish-character" of the commodity should therefore be understood not as the next step in Marx's logic, not as something that comes after section 3, "The Value-Form, or Exchange-Value" but rather as an essential part of that third section (Backhaus 1980: 102). Backhaus's arguments have often led value-form thinkers to use the first edition of Volume 1 of *Capital* in developing their readings — for one early example, see Arthur (1979) and for more in this context see Arthur's essential critique of the myth of "simple commodity production" (2005).

appearances, underlain by the true essence of human relations
(Rubin 2008: 8–9).[16]

For Rubin, this reading is not so much wrong as terribly limited and one-sided; it gets one dimension of Marx's ideas correct, yet manages to utterly miss the big picture. Rubin accepts
the view of Marx as looking past commodity relations to see
human relations behind them, but Rubin asserts that this is only
part of the story, and the other part proves far more significant
and far more surprising: "in the commodity economy, social
production relations *inevitably* took the form of things and
could not be expressed except through things. The structure of
the commodity economy *causes* things to play a particular and
highly important social role and thus to acquire particular social properties" (Rubin 2008: 9, emphasis added; see Backhaus
1980: 102).[17] Put bluntly: Marx does indeed say that the relation
between things obscures relations among people, *but that was
not his main point.* The important point for Marx was to figure
out *how* and *why* this occurred: to understand how it was that,
within capitalism, relations of production *had to take the form*
of relations between commodities; to ascertain the logic of capital itself so as to grasp how things take on social roles, functions,
and forms.[18] "Fetishism" is therefore not the name for our mysti-
fied misunderstanding of commodities as having certain social
powers, and the theory of fetishism is not designed to dispel this
illusion. The reason should now be obvious: *within capitalism,
commodities really do have such social powers.* Fetishism is not a
mistake we make as individuals — a false choice to worship false
idols; fetishism names the very structure of a capitalist social

---

16 On the important question of "essence," see Reuten 2000 and Murray 1993.

17 Rubin's account of the fetish structure of a capitalist economy recalls my
description, in the first chapter, of Salesforce CEO, Marc Benioff, forced to
"do a reset" because of a falling stock price.

18 As Backhaus puts it, "the point of the critique of political economy, however, is not the mere description of this existing fact, but the analysis of its
genesis" (Backhaus 1980: 104). I would also add that to analyze the historical
genesis of a contemporary "fact" is precisely the task of genealogy.

order. As Rubin puts it, fetishism is not "a phenomenon of social consciousness, but of social being" (Rubin 2008: 64).

What does this wider approach to the fetish have to do with the specific question of the value-form? Everything. To grasp fetishism as foundational to Marx's understanding of a capitalist social formation is to refuse to see value as a metaphysical force, a source to find or locate *outside* society. It is instead to work toward understanding the form that value takes, *and must take*, in capitalism. We can say, in short, that the misreading of Marx on value follows directly from the narrow reading of fetishism. Both interpretations are one-sided in the same problematic way: they see that Marx has identified an appearance and something that lies beneath it, but they fail to decoct from this analysis that the appearance is not false, but in fact necessary — required. Here Rubin's summary of Marx's critique of "vulgar economists" is instructive, since the misunderstanding of those economists is one shared widely today, even by self-identified Marxists:

> Vulgar economists…consider the social characteristics of things (value, money, capital, etc.) as natural characteristics which belong to the things themselves. …This is the cause of the *commodity fetishism* which is characteristics of vulgar economics. …The transformation of social production relations into social, "objective" properties of things *is a fact* about commodity-capitalist economy, and a *consequence* of the distinctive connections between the process of material production and the movement of production relations. The error of vulgar economics does not lie in the fact that it pays attention to the material forms of capitalist economy, but that it *does not see their connection with the social form* of production and *does not derive them from this social form but from the natural properties of things*. (Rubin 2008: 31, emphasis modified)

This is what Marx meant when he said, repeatedly, that the political economists had taken for granted exactly what needed to be questioned — a contention he had maintained all the way back to the so-called Paris Manuscripts (Marx 2007 [1844]: 28). The political economists (particularly the "vulgar" economists[19]) looked around themselves at what were clearly *social forms* and utterly mistook them for "eternal and natural forms" because they failed entirely to "ask themselves how these forms had originated" (Rubin 2008: 44, 45). Murray provides a powerful VFT analysis of Marx that emphasizes the "truly social" nature of Marx's account of value under capitalism. As Murray puts it, "Marx's theory of value is *nothing but his theory of the social forms* distinctive of the capitalist mode of production" (Murray 2000: 99, emphasis added).[20] The power of Marx's analysis lies in his capacity to ask the question the political economists never broached: "*why does labor assume the form of value*" (Rubin

---

19 Julie Nelson unintentionally provides a good contemporary example of the failure to see the social form that production under capitalism (i.e., production of exchange-values for the market) necessarily takes. In the context of arguing that profit should not matter that much to businesses who have a superior set of values, she writes: "market prices reflect private, not social, values" (Nelson 2006: 92). This is to make the point by getting it exactly backwards. It is not entirely clear how "value" could be a purely private thing to begin with, but even putting that aside, market prices are anything but private. To echo Rubin, the price of a gallon of gasoline is a *fact* about a particular commodity, for sale on the market, but that fact can only be established through complex systems of production, distribution, and exchange that are not only social but also cultural and political.

20 Murray's writings on Marx provide an invaluable resource for anyone trying to make sense out of Marx's understanding of the logic of capital — and beyond the terms of "worldview Marxism" (Heinrich 2012). Murray's numerous publications provide continued insights into Marx, value, and capitalism (Murray 1993, 1997, 1999, 2000, 2005). In a language that resonates throughout my work here, and which underlines the importance of value-form analysis — not just to an understanding of Marx but to an understanding of contemporary capitalist society — Murray continues his analysis (cited in the text, above) as follows: "we may speak of these forms as *value-forms*, the (generalized) commodity, money (in its several forms), capital, wage-labour, surplus-value and its forms of appearance (profit, interest, and rent), and more. The labour that produces value, then, is labour of a peculiar sort. This thought is entirely foreign to the classical labour theory of value, and, likewise, to Marxist accounts of value that mistake it for a radical version of Ricardian value theory. The gulf between the classical and the Marxian labour theories of value is wide" (Murray 2000: 99).

2008: 45, emphasis added; see Elson 1979). In asking this question, Marx breaks entirely with any standard account of the LTV; what is more, he makes it possible to rethink the relationship between value and labor under capitalism, and perhaps beyond it.

Social Forms, Social Functions_

To answer this essential question Rubin offers a deep investigation of the idea of social *forms* and the social functions they perform. A static or analytic reading of Marx always fails to grasp his understanding of the logic of capital, because for Marx a "thing" is never simply a "thing." That is to say, no entity is ever identical to itself, never the *same*, and no entity can be grasped solely in terms of its physical properties or appearances. The properties given to a thing by "nature" always drastically underdetermine it. Therefore, when Marx stresses the "two-fold" nature of the commodity, or of labor, he does not mean to say that these given, empirical objects possess two distinct properties. He means, much more literally, to suggest that sometimes they *are* one thing, and sometimes they *are* another. If I purchase a commodity for consumption — say, a hamburger — I relate to it as a use-value. The hamburger is, for me as its purchaser and consumer, a source of nutrition (debatably) and of satisfaction of my hunger (definitely). But if I own a McDonald's franchise, the hamburger is an exchange-value: I am concerned with both the number of hamburgers "produced" and sold in my store, and with my costs and revenues from the sale of hamburgers. The difference between the two examples is the difference in the "form of value," the value-form (*Wertform*). The commodity in the form of "use-value" and the commodity in the form of "exchange-value" are not the same. Marx explains that the former is the commodity's "natural form,"[21] since a hamburger would

---

21 By "natural form," Marx clearly does not mean anything like *given* in nature or *untouched* by humanity. The natural form is itself a human creation, and it depends on a prior history. Marx's point is that, if we take that

provide a hungry person needed calories in a variety of different contexts, while the latter is the "social form" since "exchange-value" *only exists* under certain, precisely structural conditions (Marx 1978).

As I have now indicated, Marx frequently uses the language of "form" in order to demonstrate the different forms of appearance of entities within capitalism. And again, Marx himself clearly recognized that the "value-form" was the most difficult idea to grasp in his entire account of capitalism (Marx 1990: 90). This may be, I submit, because the seductive powers of empiricism always tempt us to assume that what matters most is the enduring physical objectivity of an object, whereas Marx's account shows, in contrast, that what often matters most under capitalism is a form of value that can never be traced back to intrinsic physical properties. Marx's formulation of this point in *Capital* is striking: "not an atom of matter enters into the objectivity of commodities as values" (Marx 1990: 138).[22] As I write these words, crude oil has dropped to a price below $30/barrel,

---

background as given, we can then see the use-value as a "natural" thing in the sense that we can relate to it directly and *individually*: the hamburger as use-value will satisfy *my* hunger no matter how or where *I* encounter it. But the hamburger as exchange-value depends on so much more than me: changes in market supply, in consumer trends, in advertising budgets — all can affect the exchange-value of the hamburger.

22 Crucially, to say that value is not and cannot be located in the *material form* of an individual commodity is not to suggest that value is simply abstract, ideal, or non-material. Quite to the contrary, the institutions, rituals, laws, and practices of a capitalist social formation that establish the value-form are thoroughly material. Arthur helpfully articulates a related point when he explains that the value-form must not be confused for abstract value "in our heads." He writes: "one cannot just assume the substance of value and then see each commodity merely as a given magnitude, a given portion of the total value produced, for these products only become commodities with value insofar as in reality (and not 'in our heads') *exchange imposes this equivalence* on them through a material process of commensuration" (Arthur 1979: 77). Rubin, too, points to Marx's warning that we not "over-estimate" (Rubin's word) social form to such an extent that we take it to be empty (Rubin 2008: 124, 152). It is this type of untenable theoretical move that is being repeated in contemporary accounts that suggest the path to utopia lies only in imagining new forms of money (Pettifor 2014). These

after trading for most of this decade at more than $100/barrel. The point is so simple as to be easily dismissed: nothing has changed in the physical properties of a barrel of oil, and nothing has changed with respect to the oil's use-value, yet the exchange-value of oil has changed dramatically — its value-form today is radically different from two years ago.

Rubin provides a lucid explanation of Marx's account of value and the value-form by insisting that "social forms" are also "social functions." Rubin takes his cues from Marx, who, in his "Value, Price and Profit" lecture, stated directly that the "exchangeable value of commodities are only *social functions*" (Marx 1995: 13). The language of functions makes it easier to see that the supposed "same entity" can perform vastly different operations under the conditions of capitalism. Take the important but powerful example of money. Money, Marx insists, has all sorts of distinct functions (different forms), even under the terms of advanced capitalism: it can serve as measure of value, store of value, means of payment, and means of circulation (Marx 1990: chap. 3). Yet this notion of money having different functions — to allow for the circulation of goods, to pay off debts — could easily lead to the idea that I mentioned briefly in the last chapter in my discussion of Franklin: that money is merely a tool, a helpful economic instrument, and perhaps even a logical development of economic advancement in the sense that money "facilitates barter." As Murray has effectively demonstrated, this vision — shared by both classical political economy and modern economics, and also by many Marxists — could not be further from Marx's own understanding of money (Murray 2005: 50–53; see Campbell 1997; cf. Schoenberger 2008).[23]

---

thinkers are repeating Samuel Bailey's mistakes, as I briefly discussed in the preceding chapter.

23 Emphasizing precisely, à la Rubin, the importance of social form always missed by modern economics, Murray argues that "money cannot be merely an instrument in the capitalist mode of production, because money is necessary for the production of commodities and because the purpose of capitalist production, the endless accumulation of surplus value, can neither be defined nor pursued independently of money. To posit money as

Marx undermines all the instrumental accounts of money, including those that would derive money from barter, when he writes: "money is not a thing, it is a social relation" (Marx 1963 [1847]: 81). While the claim might sound odd at first — at least to economists — it makes perfect sense when read within the context of value-form analysis.[24]

For Marx, even if its material form does not change, money is not "just money"; money is a value-form, and it is the *necessary* form of appearance of value under capitalism. In just this context, Backhaus argues that "the content of Marx's form analysis is the genesis of price as price" (Backhaus 1980: 105). Backhaus here merely paraphrases Marx himself, who early on referred to price as the "peculiar form assumed by value"; indeed, "price, taken by itself, is nothing but the *monetary expression of value*" (Marx 1995: 16). Hence we have money under capitalism be-

an instrument is falsely to suppose that there could be a capitalist mode of production independent of money, to whose aid money could come" (Murray 2005: 53, citing Marx 1990: 255).

24 Marx's claim that money is a social relation also captures the core insight of the heterodox theory of money, as illuminated by Ingham's work. Marx's arguments in this context therefore also demonstrate why Ingham (2004) is too hasty to try to fit Marx into the box labelled "orthodox theory of money." It is true that Marx's writings provide neither a full history nor a sociology of money; he never develops a theory of state money, and therefore he does not fit neatly into the heterodox model that Ingham delineates. Moreover, Marx wrote *Capital* at a time when the gold standard reigned, and thus he makes the pedagogic decision to use gold as the "universal equivalent" in all his examples in that book. All of this makes it easy to miss the difference between Marx and orthodox economics, especially since later orthodox theorists, and later Marxists, all read him *as* an orthodox thinker. But Marx absolutely refuses the idea that you can have capitalist commodity exchange without money; he rejects the notion that moneyness inheres in the *functions* of money, and he utterly denies that money is ancillary or superfluous. In other words, Marx denies almost all of the fundamental tenets of an orthodox theory of money. Furthermore, Marx himself explicitly eschews one of the core tenets of orthodox theory when he ridicules the notion that money can be done away with in order to return to "simple" commodity exchange without money (Marx 1990: 149). In addition to the work of Murray (which I cite in the text), the writings of Chris Arthur (2005, 2009) and Fred Moseley and Martha Campbell (Moseley and Campbell 1997; Moseley 2005) are essential here.

cause of this value-form. Jacques Bidet refers to this phenomenon as "the inherence of money to value" (Bidet 2007: 71). Or, as
Murray puts it, in a language that resonates with the one I have
been developing here: "value and money are inseparable yet not
identical: without money there can be no value, yet money is
not value" (Murray 2005: 51; cf. Eldred and Hanlon 1981). Since
value is not an intrinsic, essential, or metaphysical substance,
there is no way that gold or Euros could literally be "value," but
value under capitalism cannot *appear* without the value-form of
money. "Not only is exchange-value the necessary form of value's appearance, money is the necessary end form of exchange-
value" (Murray 1993: 48).[25]

If "social function" must neither be reduced to nor conflated
with "instrumental use," then how do we grasp the social form/
social function of money? Perhaps a banal example can make
the point. Let us assume that I am in possession of one of those
"briefcases full of money" that always appear in the movies. My
suitcase contains bound stacks of clean, unmarked $100 bills,
totaling $100,000. From the perspective of money as a tool, I
could of course use the money for different personal ends: paying off debts, buying a Tesla, or just "making it rain." As Rubin
shows, Marx is much more interested in the social function of
elements of the capitalist social order *as they relate* to (re)pro-
duction in and of that order. In that sense, each of the above
options really amounts to consumption, $M \to C$, as the money
simply facilitates my acquisition of some use-value (in the case
of paying off debts, the consumption occurred in the past, but
the form is the same). At this point, we can dovetail our movie
example into the central example in Volume 1 of *Capital*. On the
one hand, I could hide the briefcase under a loose floorboard; on
the other, I could hand it over to a financial planner or "wealth
manager." In the first case, Marx indicates that the briefcase

---

25 Murray's claim that value and money are inseparable proves to be a radical
and contentious one within debates over interpretations of Marx. I set all
those debates aside, since within the VFT reading of Marx that I have been
developing here, the claim is much more straightforward and can easily be
traced back to Backhaus, or even to Rubin.

functions as a "hoard": the money in the briefcase serves as a basic expression of wealth for me, and in social terms it can help to facilitate a balance between the actual quantity of money in circulation and the required quantity of money (Marx 1990: 217; see Moseley 2017). In the latter case, everything changes: here and only here, *money functions as capital* and serves as one of the necessary preconditions for the general formula for capital, $M \rightarrow M'$. Money, to be clear, is not capital in and of itself: in none of the other uses for my briefcase did money appear in the form of capital or perform the social function of capital. Only when money is both excluded from consumption, yet simultaneously thrown into circulation — buying in order to sell again — does money perform the function of capital and thereby become capital. In order to *be* capital, money must *function* as capital (take the value-form of capital), and this can occur only under very specific conditions. Thus, prior to the emergence of a capitalist social order, money never functioned as capital, since that social form (and that social function) did not exist. And even within capitalism, money often fails to function as capital.[26] This discussion clarifies the main point of divergence between a value-form analysis and any sort of empiricist approach; therefore Thomas Piketty's massive project on the history of capitalism — no matter its merits — is ultimately irreconcilable with Marx because Piketty assumes that capital is an empirical object that can be statically counted and that therefore can be found at all times throughout history (Piketty 2014).[27]

---

26 Notice that the social form/function of capital is not the exclusive capacity of money: a car factory in full production is filled with capital; that same factory when taken offline during an economic downturn contains no capital. Murray pulls all the threads of this analysis together in an elliptical (Hegelian) but illuminating formulation: "as value striving to expand itself in an endless spiral, capital is not money, nor any production process, nor any commodity. ...As a category of value, capital is itself necessarily nonapparent, nonobservable, *and* it must appear as something other than itself" (Murray 1993: 58).

27 This standard approach to capital as stock — which modern Economics can trace directly back to Smith (see Mirowski 1989) — thereby has a very hard time dealing with both non-value and the destruction of value, since some-

Moreover, social functions can diverge, sometimes quite dramatically, even given the same material form. Rubin offers the example of selling cotton or selling a famous painting. In terms of the material act of exchange, we see no difference, but in terms of social function, we should observe significant divergences. Selling cotton stands apart from selling a painting because the cotton has a distinct "social nature" in terms of its overall connection, within a capitalist social order, to: (a) the conditions of production that shape that order, and (b) the conditions of reproduction of that order. Cotton is produced for exchange, and it is produced under the conditions of capitalist production: the means of production are owned by a capitalist, and the labor is wage-labor. The entire process occurs under the requirements of the production not only of cotton, but of capitalist profit.[28]

These examples help to illustrate the broader point: under capitalism, *value appears only in social form*. There is no non-

---

times capital as stock is physically destroyed (for example, during war), but often value disappears even when capital stock remains unchanged. A value-form approach can make sense of the rapid and cascading destruction of value in a crisis: if capital is a relation and not a stock, then capital (and value) simply *disappears* when the capital relation ceases to exist. Understanding the value-form thus makes perfect sense out of the paradox of capitalist crisis: when production stops, both fixed capital (factories, raw material, etc.) and variable capital (labor) go dormant at the same time (cf. Mann 2010).

28 In this example, Rubin is tacitly presuming that the painting was produced by an artist who works in isolation and owns his own paint, canvas, and other means of producing the artwork. Rubin thus takes it for granted that the art's creation was not determined by conditions of production of capitalist profit. Writing at the beginning of the twentieth century, Rubin assumes that the production of art has not been subsumed by the logic of capital, and therefore that the sale of art has a different social function than the sale of an exemplary commodity of industrial capitalism. Even today, with the subsumption of numerous sectors of the economy under the terms of capitalist production, art remains stubbornly resistant to full subsumption (although this fact does not make art immune to the forces of exchange and commodification). These main points prove central to Adorno's project and he amplifies them in great detail (Adorno 1997; Horkheimer and Adorno 2002). For detailed analysis of this peculiarity of art, see Beech 2015; see also Bernes and Spaulding 2016.

social value, no natural value — and hence, in the strict sense, no intrinsic value. Value, as Marx says repeatedly throughout *Capital*, is a social form with social functions. Capitalism is itself a structural arrangement of society — a social formation — in which value appears in the form of exchange-value (of price, of money) and in which the "source" for that value-form is the socially necessary labor-time required to produce that commodity under the prevailing conditions of that particular social order. But "socially necessary labor-time" is itself a *social form*, not a natural, technical factor that could be isolated from the social formation. Rubin formulates the general point as follows: "value is a *social form* which is acquired by the products of labor in the context of determined production relations among people" (Rubin 2008: 72). And Marx identifies socially necessary labor-time as the source of value, not in order to trace value back to a single cause — "labor-time is not the time of physics" (Bidet 2007: 70) — but rather to identify its *social nature*. This is why socially necessary labor time, and thus value, changes all the time — with changes in market conditions and, most of all, with changes in labor productivity.[29]

---

29 Like so much work in both traditional Marxism and even in the value-form tradition, I here focus mainly, as Marx does in the first volume of *Capital*, on the production of value. But as David Harvey has recently been at pains to underscore, Marx himself turns in the second volume of *Capital* to the equally important question of the *realization* of value. As Harvey puts it, "neglecting the contradictory unity of production and realization and failing to give equal weight to the content of the two volumes entails a serious misreading of Marx's theory of capital" (Harvey 2015; see Harvey 2014). I agree entirely with Harvey here, but would also emphasize that unlike a worldview Marxism, which makes labor into a transhistorical force so as to privilege value production, a genealogical and value-*form* approach to Marx poses no problem to accepting Harvey's main point. In understanding value as the value-form under capitalism, we see clearly why Marx, in moving from Volume 1 to Volume 2, would shift from production of value to its realization in exchange. Worldview Marxism must assume that value is ontologically "real" at the point of its production, and therefore, as Harvey says, realization becomes "secondary," but on a value-form reading, the social form of value is a matter just as much of realization as it is of production. Here again, Rubin's work anticipates so much that comes after. Harvey echoes Rubin, who had long ago shown both that value must be realized in

Labor and Value_

The particular implications of the claims about productivity are manifold, but let me set them aside to return to the central point that value under capitalism appears only in social form. This argument does not merely depart from the LTV; it turns it inside out. Along with many other political economists, Ricardo and Smith both endorse the general idea that labor is the source of a commodity's value; labor is the answer to where value comes from. But Ricardo and Smith, as Marx says repeatedly, mistake the *social forms* of value under capitalism for *natural forms*; hence they claim that labor's capacity to produce value is an inherent force of labor itself. It is this core idea that Marx refutes most powerfully.[30] As detailed above, for Marx there is no such thing as "labor itself"; not even "labor in general" can be mistaken for labor itself.[31] Further, the particular type of labor produced by capitalism, exchange-value-setting-labor, is above all a social form of labor. Rubin synthesizes the various strands of this analysis in order to produce a crucial, additional argument: *not* "every distribution of social labor...give[s] the product of

---

exchange and that Volume 1 was not in contradiction to the later volumes, but rather relied on different assumptions than they did (Rubin 2008: 252).

30　In addition to the many other VFT thinkers I have cited above, I would also point to the important work of Bidet, who spends a great deal of time showing why and how Marx diverges from Ricardo. In this context, Bidet makes a crucial point in relation to my broader project here, when he writes: "Ricardo sees only the quantity of value, he does not see its 'form'; he does not see that money belongs to the very nature of value. But this is above all because he does not see the substance of value (abstract labour, expenditure), of which money is the form only because its abstraction is adequate to this. *The absence of money from value in Ricardo is thus the absence of the political, of what in Marx is the presupposition of the political in value*" (Bidet 2007: 710, emphasis added).

31　The semantic differences between these two terms are, of course, quite subtle. I have tried to mark clearly the conceptual difference in my account of Marx, without introducing new terminology. Murray goes the latter route, introducing the difference between "abstract labor" and "practically abstract labor" in an effort to make Marx's value-form approach sharper and more rhetorically forceful (Murray 1999).

labor the form of value" (Rubin 2008: 72). The product of labor takes on the value-form only in the unique structure of a capitalist society in which labor is "regulated" through the force of market exchange. Rubin clarifies: other societies can produce use-values, but value in the sense of the value-form only appears when commodities are "produced specifically for sale" and then take on the value-form when they appear as exchange-value. Only a capitalist commodity economy allows for the product of labor to be/become value. The conclusion serves as both a damning repudiation of Smith and Ricardo's theories of value and, simultaneously, an opening to a novel and radical understanding of value:

> Labor does not, in itself, give value to the product, but only that *labor which is organized in a determined social form* [i.e., exchange-value-positing-labor].... If the product of labor acquires value only in a determined social form of organization of labor, then value does not represent a "property" of the product of labor, but a determined "social form" or "social function" which the product of labor fulfills as a connecting link between dissociated commodity producers, as an "intermediary" or as a "bearer" of production relations among people. (Rubin 2008: 72–73)

Here Rubin reiterates and translates a series of claims I have made above: labor does not create value; rather, exchange-value-positing-labor produces value, and the latter is not a natural entity but a social form — a highly developed social form existing only under capitalism.[32]

But Rubin goes further, and makes a consequential claim, when he draws out a point that I see as implicit but highly

---

32 Rubin nicely shows that Marx's other writings complement this broader account of value. Marx's critique of Pierre-Joseph Proudhon — and the utopian socialism that Proudhon espoused — in *The Poverty of Philosophy* (Marx 1963) treats the idea of labor-time as the determination of value *not* as "a norm of what should be" but as a fundamental articulation of the very conditions of his contemporary social order (Rubin 2008: 62).

underspecified in Marx: the question of value as a "property."
I want to unpack this point carefully, starting with Marx's discussion of the value-form in *Capital*. In what I read (indirectly
following Backhaus) as an effort to make the analysis in *Capital*
more accessible, Marx turns to a brief discussion of Aristotle
as "the first to analyse the value-form" (Marx 1990: 151). Marx
identifies Aristotle as the first thinker to grasp that exchange
renders unequal things equal; in Aristotle's equation of five
beds for one house, we therefore find an early presentation of
the equivalent form of value. Nevertheless, Marx quickly leaves
Aristotle behind, and he does so precisely because in Aristotle's
time the *social form* of value had not developed to the point that
"labor in general" could emerge. That is, the Ancient Athenian
regime lacked the social form of "exchange-value-positing-labor" because that type of labor depends upon both the ubiquity of wage-labor and the ostensible equality of all workers as
sellers of the special commodity, labor-power. Labor in Ancient
Athens was slave labor, a social form utterly distinct from, and
at odds with, exchange-value-setting-labor. Marx's treatment of
Aristotle can therefore serve as a sharp example of his refusal of
the idea of eternal "natural forms" and his consistent emphasis
on social form (cf. Murray 1999: 35).

However, this is not necessarily how Marx's short treatment
of Aristotle — or its relation to his conception of value — has
been understood by interpreters of Marx. Let me turn to a
reader from the turn of the twenty-first century, Terrell Carver, who has consistently proven himself to be a rigorous and
erudite interpreter of Marx. Carver remains unpersuaded by
Marx's account of value and he implies that the weaknesses in
Marx's analysis might be tracked back to Marx's dependence
on old ideas that he gets from Aristotle. Carver calls Aristotle
"*the* natural philosopher," and while he clearly sees that Marx
means to offer a critique of Aristotle, Carver also contends that
Marx means "to better him [Aristotle] on his [Aristotle's] own
grounds" (Carver 1998: 73). Accordingly, Carver's own presentation works backward through Marx's text, first citing Marx's
references to Aristotle's beds and houses (from late in section

3 of chapter 1) and then turning the page to Marx's very early statements on labor and value (from section 1). In other words, Carver contextualizes Marx's opening statements on labor and value as themselves answers of a sort to the problem of value as identified by Aristotle. And Carver's contextualization is neither accidental nor arbitrary, since he brings that contextualization to bear when he prefaces the key quote from section 1 by saying that "Marx's argument" here "is very much the work of an 'old-fashioned' natural philosopher" (Carver 1998: 74). The claim is not at all isolated: throughout his reading, Carver repeatedly reminds his readers that Marx's arguments on value should be read in the tradition and context of natural philosophy (Carver 1998: 70–82). Putting it all together, Carver's reader is meant to see Marx as a natural philosopher, just like *the* natural philosopher, who attempts to improve on the Aristotelian arguments relating to value.

Given this context, it is unsurprising that Carver gives an account of Marx on value wherein value does, in fact, have specific *natural properties*. Again, Carver is a learned reader of Marx, who obviously sees that Marx intends his ideas to go beyond those of Smith and Ricardo. However, when it comes to the question of value, Carver is skeptical about how far Marx really exceeds the political economists. As he puts it, Marx's "reasoning in the opening book of *Capital* is an ingeniously, but not comprehensively, critical version of arguments developed by Smith, Ricardo, and others" (Carver 1998: 79). Carver accepts the fact that Marx denies Smith's notion that "commodities *contain* value"; nevertheless, "[Marx's] own view, in my reading, was only slightly different" (Carver 1998: 79).[33] What, according to Carver, was Marx's own view? Carver asserts that, for Marx, "'[being] the products of labour' is some sort of 'property' of

---

33 Carver repeatedly suggests or implies that when it comes to the LTV, Marx was never all that far from Smith and Ricardo, claiming that Marx "relied on Ricardian propositions about value and labour," that Marx's was only the "refinement of a view held — but left unexamined — by Smith and Ricardo," and that ultimately "he and the political economists speak in [a] 'single voice'" (Carver 1998: 63, 79, 81, 82).

the 'material bodies of commodities', and so commodities are 'materialised' or 'vanished' labour or the 'static existence' of a force" (Carver 1998: 79, brackets Carver's). Put concisely, while value may not literally be "contained" in the commodity, it is a *property* of the commodity's *material body*. From here, Carver quickly moves on to his own critique of Marx.[34]

Rather than follow him there, I want to think more about the framing of Carver's interpretation, and to linger on the idea — central to all of Carver's criticisms — that value can be a "property" of commodities. First of all, let me try to contextualize Carver's own framing of Marx in terms of Marx's lineage to "old-fashioned" natural philosophy. Writing almost exactly 100 years before Carver, Eugen von Böhm-Bawerk set out a damning critique of Marx on value (Böhm-Bawerk 1949 [1896]). Rubin describes Böhm-Bawerk's work in a way that again shows the power and prescience of Rubin's overall project: "Böhm-Bawerk's arguments at first glance seem so convincing that one may boldly say that not a single later critique was formulated without repeating them" (Rubin 2008: 65). With this in mind, I will compare Carver's critique of Marx on value, with the commentary from Böhm-Bawerk. Like Carver, Böhm-Bawerk focuses intently on the opening pages of *Capital,* and like Carver, he reads those passages as *logical deductions* of labor as the source of value. Most important of all, like Carver, Böhm-Bawerk underscores the role of Aristotle, seeing Marx's text as based in, and attempting to exceed, the earlier claims of Aristotle. In the end, Böhm-Bawerk comes to the same conclusion

---

34 I have chosen to look closely at Carver's analysis because it offers both a subtle and critical engagement with Marx's account of value, and it thereby serves as the best sort of example of an interpretation of Marx that sees him still holding on to a certain conception of the LTV. Other writers are much more blunt in their assessment (and much less deft in their analysis). Steve Keen, for example, says flatly, "Marx was the greatest champion of the labor theory of value," and then he goes on to offer a critique of Marx on value (Keen 1993a; Keen 1993b; cf. Keen n.d.). For a similar example, but written more from the perspective of mainstream economics, see Wolff 1981. For a nice overview of interpretations of Marx that take him for an LTV theorist, see Rebrovick 2016.

as Carver would, writing a century later: according to Böhm-Bawerk, Marx's approach is "very old-fashioned" and Marx's logical argument for value is simply untenable (Böhm-Bawerk 1949: 68).

Responding to these arguments first requires shifting the terrain — from a tight and narrow focus on the first few lines of *Capital* to a much wider assessment of Marx's understanding of value and the value-form within the context of his broader understanding of a capitalist social formation and its historical development. Rubin opens section 2 of his book by mapping out just this topography:

> In the first pages of *Capital*, Marx, by means of the *analytic* method, passes from exchange value to value, and from value to labor. But the complete *dialectical* ground of Marx's theory of value can only be given on the basis of his theory of commodity fetishism which analyzes the general structure of the commodity economy. Only after one finds the basis of Marx's theory of value does it become clear what Marx says in the famous first chapter of *Capital*. Only then do Marx's theory of value as well as numerous critiques of it appear in a proper light. ...The point of departure of the labor theory of value is a determined social environment, a society with a determined production structure. (Rubin 2008: 65)

When Rubin distinguishes between "analytic" and "dialectical" he is not just waving his hands — in the way some Marxists have been known to do — about the magical power of the Marxist dialectic. To the contrary, Rubin is referring explicitly and concretely to Marx's comments in the *1857 Introduction* — that is, the introduction to *Zur Kritik*[35] — about what distinguishes

---

35 The *1857 Introduction* is a draft manuscript, titled "Introduction," from one of Marx's notebooks (Labelled "M") dated to late 1857. In the preface to *Zur Kritik*, which he published just two years later, Marx refers to this manuscript and explains that he decided to omit it from the final text (*Zur Kritik* has no introduction). When *Zur Kritik* was first published in English

Marx's approach to economic forms from the method of the political economists. The political economists *start* with given social forms, but take them to be given by *nature*, not by history. This starting point leads the political economists to attempt to *reduce* those forms to a "material-technical basis or content" (Rubin 2008: 46; cf. Marx 1990: 148; Marx 1996: 150). Marx calls this process of reasoning *analytic*, and he contrasts it with a "genetic" approach — a dynamic, *dialectical* approach — that begins with a given social form *as social* (as historically produced) and then attempts to unravel that social form, to explain its character and development (Rubin 2008: 46). In the case of the question of the relation of labor and value, this means starting with the *social fact* that under capitalism, commodities (creations of a specific production process) can be exchanged for one another; from this basis one can then ask how it is that the form of value in such a social order is *required* to take the shape that it does. In this way, we might well say, as Rubin does above, that Marx has a "labor theory of value." But that theory is not designed to trace the transhistorical source of value back to *labor itself*; rather, such a theory inquires after the conditions that would

---

translation in 1904, this manuscript from 1857 was included as an appendix. Based on these straightforward reasons, I have argued elsewhere in some detail that it makes the most sense to understand the *1857 Introduction* as an unpublished introduction to *Zur Kritik* (Chambers 2014: 88–91). However, the middle decades of the twentieth century saw the appearance of the *Grundrisse,* an editorial construction derived from Marx's notebooks from the 1850s, yet presented primarily by editors and commentators as a lost "book" by Marx. In this presentation, the *1857 Introduction* appears as the introduction to that putative book. Over the years the *Grundrisse* has come to be taken as one of Marx's most important works, and therefore the idea that the *1857 Introduction* properly belongs to that book has become normalized. Even standalone translations of the text now refer to it as "*Introduction* to the *Grundrisse*" (Carver 1975; Carver 1996). The dominance of this approach to the text explains the need for detail in my earlier work on the *1857 Introduction*, which I rest upon here when I say in my text above that the manuscript is actually best understood as an unpublished introduction to *Zur Kritik*. For a subtle and sophisticated discussion of the *1857 Introduction* in relation to *Zur Kritik*, the *Grundrisse,* and Marx's larger project, see Heinrich 2009: 79–81.

make it possible for value to *take the form* of exchange-value, as itself the product of socially-necessary labor time — all of which can and does only occur under the specific conditions of capitalist production.[36]

This account leads to the conclusion that — contra Böhm-Bawerk, contra Carver, and contra Aristotle — whatever we might say about "value," we cannot adequately render it as a "property" of the commodity.[37] Rubin provides the perfect pedagogical explanation by using a heuristic that cuts directly against an Aristotelian, natural philosophy approach. That is, his example *sounds like* the type that Aristotle himself would use, while actually revealing the wide gap between Marx's way of thinking and that of so-called natural philosophy. Rubin asks us to consider "a painted, round oak table [that] costs, or has the value of 25 roubles" (Rubin 2008: 73). Rubin then explains the obvious: according to the grammatical and logical terms of the sentence, it seems to provide information on "four properties of the table." But, I might add, we only see it this way because of what Nietzsche calls the "metaphysical seduction of grammar," which tempts us to believe that the structure and rules of

---

36 This context helps to illuminate one of the most powerful yet opaque lines in Backhaus's early work: "abstract value objectiveness (*Wertgegenstandlichkeit*) is for Marx social objectivity par excellence" (Backhaus 1980: 112).

37 In the main text, below, I work through this logic by following Rubin's account, but it seems worth emphasizing that even in chapter 1 of Volume 1 of *Capital*, Marx himself underlines the point that "value" is not a natural property of commodities. Perhaps he is nowhere more emphatic than in specifying the *limitations* to the analogy he himself draws between the value-form and weight. In his effort to explain the relative and equivalent value-forms — in which one commodity represents the *value* of another — Marx has recourse to the idea of weights on a scale, in which an iron weight represents the weight of a loaf of bread. Marx then writes: "In the expression of the weight of the sugar-loaf, the iron represents a natural property common to both bodies, their weight; but in the expression of value of the linen *the coat represents a supra-natural property*: their value, *which is something purely social*" (Marx 1990: 148, emphasis added). When I say that three pairs of socks are "worth" one shirt, the value that the shirt represents absolutely cannot be found in the material body of the shirt; its value is not a natural property of the shirt.

language reflect the nature of reality (Nietzsche 1967: 45). But in the case of the twenty-five-rouble, painted, round oak table, one of the so-called *properties* is nothing at all like the others. The properties of being painted, round, and made of oak are all *material* properties of the "natural form" of the table. But the "property" of having an exchange-value of twenty-five roubles is really *no property at all*. This exchange-value is itself the *social form* of the table, under the conditions of capitalism. To say the table has a price of twenty-five roubles is to say that "it is produced for the market, that its producer is related to other members of society by production relations among commodity owners, that the economy has a determined social form, namely the form of commodity economy" (Rubin 2008: 73). In telling us that the table has a price of twenty-five roubles, "we do not learn anything about the technical aspects of the production or about the thing itself, but we learn something about the social form of the production" (Rubin 2008: 73).

This account brings us to a decisive point: *value can never be a property*. The difficulty with value, as I would put it, is that we always want to see it as a property of a thing (if not, as in Smith, the actual content of a thing), but it is neither a property nor an "expression." Value is always the *manifestation* of a social form. Rubin insists that "value does not characterize things, but human relations." Further, value "is not a property of things but a social form acquired by things" (Rubin 2008: 73). Value is a form of appearance within a social order; it is always, only and ever, a social form. In this context, Rubin implicitly offers what we might call his working definition of value. Quoting Marx, he writes: "value is a 'social relation taken as a thing', a production relation among people which takes the form of a property of things" (Rubin 2008: 73, citing Marx 2009: 11). Here Rubin zeroes in on exactly the idea in Marx upon which I centered my reading of *Zur Kritik* in the previous chapter — the central claim that *Tauschwert setzende Arbeit* is "a specific social form of labor" (Marx 2009: 11). Echoing my earlier discussion, Rubin even emphasizes that the idea of labor "creating" value is not quite right, suggesting that "determines" is a better translation for *setzende*. My own way of formulating the general point would be to maintain the key distinction between, on the one hand, thinking of value as a "property" of some entity and, on the other, grasping value in both the broadest and deepest sense as a social form.

By always bearing this overarching point in mind, while also considering Marx's account in its broad, dialectical sense, we can easily construct a response to Carver, and Böhm-Bawerk before him. Both find hollow and dissatisfying (Carver calls it "circular") the idea that abstract labor somehow serves as the "common substance" that equalizes both the exchange of commodities and the various concrete forms of labor that produces those commodities (Böhm-Bawerk 1949: 68; Carver 1998: 76). But we can now see that Marx, too, would (in fact, *did*) find such an argument inadequate, and that he himself never espouses it. Rubin argues as follows:

> [A]bstract labor is a social and historical concept. *Abstract labor does not express a psychological equality of various forms of labor, but **a social equalization** of different forms of labor which is realized in the specific form of equalization of the products of labor.* The special character of Marx's theory of value consists of the fact that it **explained precisely the kind of labor that creates value.** (Rubin 2008: 75, italics Rubin's, bolded text mine)

What "kind of labor creates value"? Exchange-value-positing-labor, itself the achievement of the development of a capitalist social order. The answer to the question of "common substance" (that which renders commodities equal under capitalism) is not, therefore, to be provided *analytically by Marx* (Rubin 2008: 138). To read him this way is to miss the point of his entire approach. The answer to that question is provided *dialectically by the historical development of a capitalist social formation.* "What renders commodities equal?" is not a philosophical question, but an historical one. And therefore the answer cannot simply be "labor." That would amount to an analytic or philosophical answer that posits "labor itself" as having the "property" of "producing value." The answer must be an historical, genealogical one: under capitalism, labor creates value, but only the abstract labor (labor in general), a highly developed social form achieved by capitalist historical development. Exchange-value-positing-labor is "precisely the kind of labor that creates value."

Capitalism and the Value-Form_

When it comes to the question of value (in relation to labor) under capitalism, Marx's task is therefore not to "find the right answer," but to analyze, to deconstruct, and reconstruct the very answer that the historical development of capitalist social formations has already provided in definite form. Rubin brings out this decisive notion by arguing that to understand capitalism we have to deal directly with "the entire *mechanism which connects value and labor*" (Rubin 2008: 78). In other words, value is not traced to labor by way of a metaphysics, but through the system of capitalist production, distribution, exchange, and consumption — that is, through political economy itself. Like all "laws" of political economy, the so-called labor theory of value is therefore not Marx's "theory," and in a way, it is not even Smith and Ricardo's; it is capitalism's theory.[38]

The value-form approach dovetails with the genealogical reading of Marx in my previous chapter, since both allow us to see that Marx is *diagnosing* the LTV, not arguing for, or even

---

38 Rubin himself holds on to the nomenclature by which Marx himself "has" a labor theory of value. But as should be plainly evident by now, Rubin's reading of Marx on value has thoroughly resignified the meaning of such a claim. Indeed, for Rubin, what we would call "Marx's LTV" is not even really about labor or value; instead, it concerns the fetishism of both, achieved as an actual fact by capitalism. "The labor theory of value did not discover the material condensation of labor (as a factor of production) in things which are the products of labor; this takes place in all economic formations and is the technical basis of value, but not its cause. The labor theory of value discovered the fetish, the reified expression of social labor in the value of things. Labor is 'crystallized' or formed in value in the sense that it acquires the social 'form of value'" (Rubin 2008: 76).

against it. Marx's central claim is that value under capitalism appears only in social form; his critique of classical political economy pivots on the demonstration that the classical economists repeatedly mistake social forms for natural forms. Yet, in showing that the value-form is a social form, Marx is not denying the concrete reality of that form of value — just the opposite. This makes Marx's critique of political economy much more radical than it would be under a standard reading (in which Marx repeats the substantialist LTV but in doing so affirms the importance of labor). Marx's refutation takes shape as a genealogical unwinding of the LTV — a taking-apart that shows how it was put together. Marx has no labor theory of value because he has no "theory of value" (nor a "theory of labor") in the narrow sense of an objective theory that would trace value to its ahistorical source (cf. Postone 1993).

To see Marx as genealogist is thus also to see why the marginalist critique of the classical value theory is not a critique of Marx. Neoclassical economics, of course, does away with the LTV and purports to do away with value theory itself. Rather than entrenching the LTV as a founding tale (a good myth) it discards it as an outdated and entirely false theory (a bad myth). Thorstein Veblen coined the term "neo-classical school" in order, first, to *minimize* the gap between contemporary competing schools — Marshall's marginalism on the one hand, and the "Austrian school" on the other — as "scarcely distinguishable," and second, to *maximize* the gap between these schools and both "the historical and Marxist schools" (Veblen 1900: 261). This second gap, Veblen emphasizes, "is wider, so much so, indeed, as to bar out a consideration of the postulates of the latter under the same head of inquiry with the former" (Veblen 1900: 261). Veblen here makes two important moves at once: he lumps Marx in with the classical political economists,[39] right be-

---

39 Mirowski, a strong admirer of both Veblen's work and of the broader project of early twentieth-century institutionalist economics, develops a number of crucial insights from Veblen, but he also repeats Veblen's error in failing to see that Marx's account of value is not the same as that of classical political economy (Mirowski 1988; Mirowski 1989).

fore tossing the entire lot aside as simply incomparable with the work being done in early twentieth-century economics. Marx thus becomes a supporter of the LTV just as the LTV is turned into nothing more than a fairytale.

However, we have now seen that Marx is not a theorist of labor or value, but a genealogist of the form of value as it emerges within particular social orders. As such a thinker, Marx clearly can neither affirm nor simply reject the LTV. To read Marx genealogically is thus to make sense out of his rather *peculiar* emphasis on both the concept of "the social" and the word *social*. As I highlighted in the previous chapter, Marx initiates his genealogy by giving Petty credit for an inchoate understanding of the "social aspect" of the commodity. His account of Petty echoes Marx's own frequent repetition of this theme in the chapter on "The Commodity" in *Zur Kritik*. There, Marx underscores "the specific way in which exchange-value-setting-labor, that is commodity-producing-labor, is *social labor*" (Marx 2009: 7–8, my translation). And as Bonefeld, Gunn, and Psychopedis show, all categories of the value-form "are social categories, and *vice versa*"; moreover, as social categories, they are, even in their abstract form, manifested in concrete reality, not just in thought (Bonefeld, Gunn, and Psychopedis 1992: xviii).

The fact that Marx did not subscribe to classical value theory, but instead utterly displaced it in his analysis of the genetic development of the capitalist social order — this fact fundamentally alters our interpretation of Marx. But it should also force us to rethink our relation to the logic of capital by changing the way we conceptualize the capital–value relation. That is, if exchange-value is the *necessary* form of appearance of value under capitalism, then to take an approach to capitalism inspired by Marx's analysis means to refuse the idea of locating value outside the social formation.[40] In the closing line of his early article on the

---

40 I call this an analysis "inspired by Marx," but not necessarily Marxist, since that term seems too fraught and freighted and because so much of my interpretation of Marx is at odds with various "Marxist" readings. I should also stress that the refusal to locate value outside the social order does not

value-form, Arthur sums this point up powerfully when he says: "value emerges from the dialectical relations of commodity exchange; it is not an abstract essence inhering in a product in a pseudo-natural fashion" (Arthur 1979: 80). But if value only *emerges* from social relations within a concrete social order, then we must utterly reconsider the notion of intrinsic value: a society's values cannot be independent of the social order itself. Rather than serve as cause for that social order, those values must emanate from within it. The source of value does not lie with an external cause that provides a metaphysical grounding; the social formation is itself the structural "cause" of the production of value.[41]

This insight helps to explain why Marx was so very critical of what he saw as "ethical critiques" of capitalism, like those made by Proudhon and so many other utopian socialists (Marx 1963; cf. Chambers 2014: 15–16). One does not oppose the logic of capital by offering up moral plaints. This perspective throws my telling of the Wells Fargo story, from my first chapter, into stark

---

reduce to relativism, since as Marx so deftly shows, there is nothing random or arbitrary about value under capitalism.

41 The language of "cause" only appears problematic because certain (positivistic) epistemologies insist on the narrow idea that a cause must be wholly independent from its effect (hence *independent* and *dependent* variables). But this approach to causality has been thoroughly discredited by a whole host of diverse epistemological and ontological alternatives, numerous of which have nothing to do with Marx or Marxism (for a powerful contribution to these arguments, see Connolly 2011; Connolly 2013). Moreover, the logic by which a "structural cause" amounts to so-called determinism depends upon the same sort of bankrupt logic. Structuralism = determinism is written on the obverse side of the coin that is headed with I→D (a formula that concisely expresses the idea that all explanation must stem from an independent variable *causing* effects on a dependent variable). Therefore, only an ungenerous and reductive reading will conclude that locating the source of value *within* the social formation leads to some sort of nihilistic determinism. Determinists, I submit, are a lot like relativists, as aptly described by Richard Rorty: aside from the most exotic of environs, one never actually locates them outside of the academic laboratory (Rorty 1982). (Rorty says we only find "relativists" in first-year University Philosophy classes; I would suggest, in turn, that we only run across "determinists" in the hyperbolic rhetoric of certain twentieth-century Marxist discourses).

relief. In particular, we see that the project of a "moral economy," understood as an effort to develop something like "*just economic theory*" is quite plainly bankrupt from the start. The philosopher who generates new values or new "normative principles" directly from his or her brain, or indirectly from philosophical schemata or programs, will always be helpless when facing a social order that generates its values through concrete material practice. Marx's lifelong study of the capitalist value-form demonstrates the impossibility of offering a transformative critique of capitalism by opposing a new set of values from the outside. The reason why is crucial: *capitalism does not offer a choice of value-systems; it produces and imposes its own.* Therefore the only way to oppose capitalism is to undo and to remake its structures, not to value those structures or their effects differently. The latter turns out to be a definitional impossibility once we understand how the logic of capital works within a concrete social order.[42]

This brings me back to one of my central claims of this book: the discussion of value is not supplemental but rather essential to any politico-economic project, for the precise reason that one of the most important things capitalism does is establish value. This indispensable point has been consistently overlooked by so many writers — modern economists, political theorists, and also Marxists. Marx's ideas on value have been neglected, dismissed, or wrongly defended because his genealogical diagnosis of classical value theory and his development of a theory of value-form were collapsed together and misinterpreted as mere repetitions of a classical theory of value. Marx was thus taken to offer a minor, internal challenge to classical political economy, one that operated on its own terrain. But as we have now seen,

---

42 There is no denying the long history of self-avowed Marxists who saw their central principle as that of revaluing labor, of honoring the dignity and worth of labor in the face of capitalist society's ostensible denigration of it. Despite their prevalence and their historical and political importance, all such projects depart radically from Marx's account of the value-form, since it is the capitalist social formation itself that makes labor (of a particular sort) the source of value.

Marx's critique of classical political economy hinged on rethinking value in a social order entirely,[43] and therefore on demonstrating that value is itself a political category (Bidet 2007: 67). Working out and then greatly advancing Rubin's logic, I have shown here that Marx provides an entirely different way to understand value in the first place. And in so doing, he may have been the only thinker to explain, deeply and thoroughly, how value works under capitalism. Once we understand the value-form as a product of a capitalist social formation, we can quickly see that value is socio-political, and, in the same way, a capitalist social order is politico-economic.[44] As a social form (as value-form), value cannot be confined to any particular domain within the social order; value is a constitutive element of the social order itself. Changed or new values can therefore only become possible through social transformation, which itself must critically engage with the logic of capital.

---

43 If Marx were simply modifying the LTV, then his work on this front would prove insignificant or dismissible, given that today no one really buys into any sort of labor theory of value. In other words, if the marginalists' answer to the question of value proves valid, then disputes between Marx and Ricardo over labor are utterly superfluous.

44 Here I draw on Bidet's formulation of value as "sociopolitical." Bidet extends this analysis to demonstrate the deep mutual imbrication of "politics" and "economics." He writes: "the novelty of the categorical configuration introduced by Marx, in my view, is something quite different from the trivial idea that labour relations are also power relations. It effects a coupling of economic and political categories at the most fundamental level, in such a way that these two orders cannot then be completely dissociated: the economic category of labour-value is only a semi-concept, lacking operational value, outside of this concept of 'consumption', i.e. a definite type of social compulsion to produce" (Bidet 2007: 51).

Bibliography_

Adorno, Theodor. 1997. *Aesthetic Theory,* trans. Robert Hullot-Kentor. Minneapolis: University of Minnesota Press.

Allan, Bentley B. 2018. *Scientific Cosmology and International Orders.* Cambridge: Cambridge University Press; https://doi.org/10.1017/9781108241540.

Althusser, Louis. 1969. *For Marx,* trans. Ben Brewster. London: Verso.

Arthur, Christopher J. 1979. "Dialectic of the Value-Form." In *Value: The Representation of Labour in Capitalism,* ed. Diane Elson, 67–81. London: C.S.E. Books.

———. 2004. *The New Dialectic and Marx's Capital.* Leiden: Brill.

———. 2005. "The Myth of 'Simple Commodity Production.'" *Marx Myths & Legends.* http://marxmyths.org/chris-arthur/article2.htm.

———. 2009. "The Concept of Money." In *Karl Marx and Contemporary Philosophy,* eds. Andrew Chitty and Martin McIvor, 159–73. London: Palgrave Macmillan.

Atwater, Peter. 2016. "Maximizing Shareholder Value May Have Gone Too Far." *Time,* June 3, http://time.com/4355685/maximizing-shareholder-value/.

Backhaus, Hans-Georg. 1980. "On the Dialectics of the Value-Form." *Thesis Eleven* 1, no. 1: 99–120; https://doi.org/10.1177/072551368000100108.

————. 1997. *Dialektik der Wertform: Untersuchungen zur Marxschen Ökonomiekritik.* Freiburg: ça ira–Verlag.

Bailey, Samuel. 1825. *A Critical Dissertation on the Nature, Measures, and Causes of Value.* London: R. Hunter.

Bakan, Joel. 2012. *The Corporation: The Pathological Pursuit of Profit and Power.* London: Constable & Robinson Ltd.

Beech, Dave. 2015. *Art and Value: Art's Economic Exceptionalism in Classical, Neoclassical and Marxist Economics.* Leiden: Brill.

Bellofiore, Riccardo and Tommaso Redolfi Riva. 2015. "The *Neue Marx-Lektüre*: Putting the Critique of Political Economy Back into the Critique of Society." *Radical Philosophy* 189 (Jan/Feb): 24–36; https://www.radicalphilosophyarchive.com/article/the-neue-marx-lekture.

Benioff, Marc. 2015. "A Call for Stakeholder Activists." *Huffington Post,* February 2, http://www.huffingtonpost.com/marc-benioff/a-call-for-stakeholder-activists_b_6599000.html.

Benner, Katie and Leslie Picker. 2016. "Salesforce Shareholders Besiege Possible Twitter Deal." *The New York Times,* October 7, https://www.nytimes.com/2016/10/08/technology/salesforce-shareholders-besiege-possible-twitter-deal.html.

Bernes, Jasper and Daniel Spaulding. 2016. "Truly Extraordinary." Review of *Art and Value: Art's Economic Exceptionalism in Classical, Neoclassical and Marxist Economics,* by Dave Beech. *Radical Philosophy* 195 (Jan/Feb): 51–54; https://www.radicalphilosophy.com/reviews/individual-reviews/truly-extraordinary.

Bidet, Jacques. 2007. *Exploring Marx's* Capital: *Philosophical, Economic and Political Dimensions,* trans. David Fernbach. Leiden: Brill.

Blodget, Henry. 2012. "We Need To Stop Maximizing Profit And Start Maximizing Value." *Business Insider,* December 8, http://www.businessinsider.com/lets-stop-maximizing-profit-and-start-maximizing-value-2012-12.

Blyth, Mark. 2013. *Austerity: The History of a Dangerous Idea.* Oxford: Oxford University Press.

Boer, Roland. 2010. "That Hideous Pagan Idol: Marx, Fetishism and Graven Images." *Critique* 38, no. 1: 93–116; https://doi.org/10.1080/03017600903454413.

Böhm-Bawerk, Eugen von. 1949. *Karl Marx and the Close of His System.* New York: Augustus M. Kelley Publishers.

Bonefeld, Werner. 1998. Review of *Dialektik der Wertform,* by Hans-Georg Backhaus. *Capital & Class* 22, no. 3: 158–61.

Bonefeld, Werner, Richard Gunn, and Kosmas Psychopedis. 1992. Introduction to *Open Marxism, Volume I: Dialectics and History,* eds. Werner Bonefeld, Richard Gunn, and Kosmas Psychopedis, ix–xx. London: Pluto Press.

Campbell, Martha. 1997. "Marx's Theory of Money: A Defense." In *New Investigations of Marx's Method,* eds. Fred Moseley and Martha Campbell, 89–120. Atlantic Highlands: Humanities Press.

Cantillon, Richard. 1755. *Essai sur la nature du commerce en général.* London: Chez Fletcher Gyles.

Carver, Terrell. 1998. *The Postmodern Marx.* Manchester: Manchester University Press.

———. 2003. *Engels: A Very Short Introduction.* Oxford: Oxford University Press.

Carver, Terrell and Daniel Blank. 2014a. *A Political History of the Editions of Marx and Engels's "German Ideology Manuscripts."* New York: Palgrave Macmillan.

———. 2014b. *Marx and Engels's "German Ideology" Manuscripts: Presentation and Analysis of the "Feuerbach Chapter."* New York: Palgrave Macmillan.

CCCF (Capital Community College Foundation). 2016. "Guide to Grammar and Writing." http://grammar.ccc.commnet.edu/grammar/.

CFPB (Consumer Financial Protection Bureau). 2016. "Consumer Financial Protection Bureau Fines Wells Fargo $100 Million for Widespread Illegal Practice of Secretly Opening Unauthorized Accounts." September 8, https://www.consumerfinance.gov/about-us/newsroom/consumer-financial-protection-bureau-fines-wells-fargo-100-million-widespread-illegal-practice-secretly-opening-unauthorized-accounts/.

Chambers, Samuel A. 2001. "Foucault's Evasive Maneuvers: Nietzsche, Interpretation, Critique." *Angelaki: Journal of Theoretical Humanities* 6, no. 3: 101–23; https://doi.org/10.1080/09697250120087978.

———. 2009. *The Queer Politics of Television*. London: I.B. Tauris.

———. 2014. *Bearing Society in Mind: Theories and Politics of the Social Formation*. London: Rowman & Littlefield International.

———. 2017. "What Kind of Theory is the Labor Theory of Value? Marx as Genealogist in *Zur Kritik*." *Political Power and Social Theory* 32: 63–98; https://doi.org/10.1108/S0198-871920170000032004.

"Chief Executive Officer." 2018. *Wikipedia*, https://en.wikipedia.org/wiki/Chief_executive_officer.

Clarke, J.B. 1946. "Distribution." In *Readings in The Theory of Income Distribution,* ed. Frank E. Norton, 58–71. Philadelphia: Blakiston Company.

Cohen, Gerald A. 1979. "The Labor Theory of Value and the Concept of Exploitation." *Philosophy and Public Affairs* 8, no. 4: 338–60; http://www.jstor.org/stable/2265068.

Connolly, William E. 1987. *Politics and Ambiguity*. Madison: The University of Wisconsin Press.

———. 2011. *A World of Becoming*. Durham: Duke University Press.

———. 2013. *The Fragility of Things: Self-organizing Processes, Neoliberal Fantasies, and Democratic Activism*. Durham: Duke University Press.

Cook, Deborah. 1990. "Nietzsche and Foucault on *Ursprung* and Genealogy." *Clio: A Journal of Literature History and the Philosophy of History* 19, no. 4: 299–309.

Corkery, Michael. 2016a. "Elizabeth Warren Accuses Wells Fargo Chief of 'Gutless Leadership'." *The New York Times,* September 20, https://www.nytimes.com/2016/09/21/business/dealbook/wells-fargo-ceo-john-stumpf-senate-testi-mony.html.

———. 2016b. "Wells Fargo Fined $185 Million for Fraudulently Opening Accounts." *The New York Times,* September 8, https://www.nytimes.com/2016/09/09/business/dealbook/wells-fargo-fined-for-years-of-harm-to-customers.html.

Cowley, Stacy. 2016. "Wells Fargo Workers Claim Retaliation for Playing by the Rules." *The New York Times,* September 26, https://www.nytimes.com/2016/09/27/business/dealbook/wells-fargo-workers-claim-retaliation-for-playing-by-the-rules.html.

Davis, Nathaniel B. 2016. "If War Can Have Ethics, Wall Street Can, Too." *The New York Times,* October 3, https://www.nytimes.com/2016/10/03/opinion/if-war-can-have-ethics-wall-street-can-too.html.

Debreu, Gérard. 1959. *Theory of Value: An Axiomatic Analysis of Economic Equilibrium.* New York: Wiley.

Denning, Steve. 2014. "JPMorgan Embraces 'The World's Dumbest Idea.'" *Forbes,* December 26, https://www.forbes.com/sites/stevedenning/2014/12/26/jp-morgan-embraces-the-worlds-dumbest-idea/.

———. 2015. "Salesforce CEO Slams 'The World's Dumbest Idea': Maximizing Shareholder Value." *Forbes,* February 5, https://www.forbes.com/sites/stevedenning/2015/02/05/salesforce-ceo-slams-the-worlds-dumbest-idea-maximizing-shareholder-value/.

Dobb, Maurice. 1973. *Theories of Value and Distribution Since Adam Smith: Ideology and Economic Theory.* Cambridge: Cambridge University Press.

Dodd-Frank Wall Street Reform and Consumer Protection Act of 2010, Pub. L. No. 111–203, 124 Stat. 1376 (2010).

Eldred, Michael and Marnie Hanlon. 1981. "Reconstructing Value-Form Analysis." *Capital & Class* 5, no. 1: 24–60; https://doi.org/10.1177/030981688101300103.

Eldred, Michael and Mike Roth. 1980. Translators' Introduction to Hans-Georg Backhaus, "On the Dialectics of the

Value Form." *Thesis Eleven* 1, no. 1: 94–98; https://doi.org/10.1177/072551368000100106.

Elson, Diane. 1979. Value: *The Representation of Labour in Capitalism.* London: C.S.E. Books.

"Equivocate." 2015. *New Oxford American Dictionary.* 3rd edn., eds. Angus Stevenson and Christine A. Lindberg. Oxford: Oxford University Press.

Foucault, Michel. 1972. *The Archaeology of Knowledge,* trans. A.M. Sheridan Smith. New York: Pantheon Books.

———. 1984. *The Foucault Reader,* ed. Paul Rabinow. New York: Pantheon Books.

Gandel, Stephen. 2016. "Wells Fargo Exec Who Headed Phony Accounts Unit Collected $125 Million." *Fortune,* September 12, http://fortune.com/2016/09/12/wells-fargo-cfpb-carrie-tolstedt/.

Glynos, Jason and David R. Howarth. 2007. *Logics of Critical Explanation in Social and Political Theory.* London: Routledge.

Halperin, David M. 2002. *How to Do the History of Homosexuality.* Chicago: University of Chicago Press.

Harvey, David. 1982. *The Limits to Capital.* Chicago: University of Chicago Press.

———. 2014. *Seventeen Contradictions and the End of Capitalism.* Oxford: Oxford University Press.

———. 2015. "'The Most Dangerous Book I Have Ever Written': A Commentary on *Seventeen Contradictions and the End of Capitalism.*" *Reading Marx's* Capital *with David Harvey,* May 19, http://davidharvey.org/2015/05/the-most-dangerous-book-i-have-ever-written-a-commentary-on-seventeen-contradictions-and-the-end-of-capitalism/.

Heinrich, Michael. 2009. "Reconstruction or Deconstruction? Methodological Controversies about Value and Capital, and New Insights from the Critical Edition." In *Re-reading Marx: New Perspectives after the Critical Edition,* eds. Riccardo Bellofiore and Roberto Fineschi, 71–98. London: Palgrave Macmillan.

————. 2012. *An Introduction to the Three Volumes of Karl Marx's* Capital, trans. Alexander Locascio. New York: Monthly Review Press.

Horkheimer, Max. 1999. "Traditional and Critical Theory." In *Critical Theory: Selected Essays,* trans. M. O'Connell, 188–243. New York: Continuum Press.

Horkheimer, Max and Theodor W. Adorno. 2002. *Dialectic of Enlightenment: Philosophical Fragments,* ed. Gunzelin Schmid Noerr, trans. Edmund Jephcott. Stanford: Stanford University Press.

Huber, Matthew T. 2017. "Value, Nature and Labor: A Defense of Marx." *Capitalism Nature Socialism* 28, no. 1: 39–52, https://doi.org/10.1080/10455752.2016.1271817.

Ingham, Geoffrey. 2004. *The Nature of Money.* Cambridge: Polity Press.

Isaac, Mike, Katie Benner, and Michael J. de la Merced. 2016. "Twitter Is Said to Be Discussing a Possible Takeover." *The New York Times,* September 23, https://www.nytimes.com/2016/09/24/business/dealbook/twitter-sale.html.

Jevons, William Stanley. 1971. *The Theory of Political Economy.* New York: Penguin Books.

Keen, Steve. 1993a. "Use-Value, Exchange Value and the Demise of Marx's Labor Theory of Value." *Journal of the History of Economic Thought* 15, no. 1: 107–21; https://doi.org/10.1017/S1053837200005290.

————. 1993b. "The Misinterpretation of Marx's Theory of Value." *Journal of the History of Economic Thought* 15, no. 2: 282–300; https://doi.org/10.1017/S1053837200000985.

————. [n.d.] "A Marx for Post Keynesians" Unpublished paper. Accessed September 12, 2017, http://keenomics.s3.amazonaws.com/debtdeflation_media/papers/Amfpk.pdf

Keynes, John Maynard. 1964. *The General Theory of Employment, Interest, and Money.* London: Macmillan.

Kim, Eugene. 2016. "These Comments by Salesforce CEO Marc Benioff Convinced Investors He's Not Buying Twitter — And the Stock is Popping." *Business Insider,* October

6, http://www.businessinsider.com/salesforce-ceo-marc-benioff-not-buying-twitter-2016-10.

Kliman, Andrew. 2007. *Reclaiming Marx's* Capital: *A Refutation of the Myth of Inconsistency.* Lanham: Lexington Books.

Larsen, Niel, Mathias Nilges, Josh Robinson, and Nicholas Brown. 2014. *Marxism and the Critique of Value.* Chicago: MCM' Publishing.

"Law." *Oxford English Dictionary.* Accessed September 18, 2016. http://www.oed.com.

Leswing, Kif. 2016. "Apple Just Reported the Largest Quarterly Profit in History." *Business Insider,* January 26, http://www.businessinsider.com/apple-sets-record-quarterly-profit-2016-1.

Lopez, Linette. 2016. "Here's Why it Seems like the CEO of Wells Fargo Can't Remember Anything." *Business Insider,* September 20, http://www.businessinsider.com/why-wells-fargos-stumpf-cant-remember-much-about-what-happened-2016-9.

Mandel, Ernest. 1990. Introduction, *Capital: A Critique of Political Economy,* Vol. 1, ed. Ben Fowkes, 11–86. New York: Penguin Books.

Mann, Geoffrey. 2010. "Value After Lehman." *Historical Materialism* 18, no. 4: 172–88; https://doi.org/10.1163/156920610X550640.

Marx, Karl. 1904. *A Contribution to the Critique of Political Economy,* trans. N.I. Stone. Chicago: Charles H. Kerr & Company.

———. 1963. *The Poverty of Philosophy,* trans. Institute of Marxism Leninism. New York: International Publishers.

———. 1969a. *Theories of Surplus Value, Part 1,* ed. S. Ryazanskaya. London: Lawrence & Wishart.

———. 1969b. *Theories of Surplus Value, Part 2,* ed. S. Ryazanskaya. London: Lawrence & Wishart.

———. 1975. *Karl Marx: Texts on Method,* ed. Terrell Carver. Oxford: Basil Blackwell.

———. 1978. "The Value-Form," trans. Mike Roth and Wal Suchting. *Capital and Class* 2, no. 1: 134–50; https://doi.org/1 0.1177/030981687800400110.

———. 1990. *Capital: A Critique of Political Economy,* Vol. 1, trans. Ben Fowkes. New York: Penguin Books.

———. 1995. *Value, Price and Profit,* ed. Eleanor Marx Aveling. New York: International Co. Inc.

———. 1996. *Later Political Writings,* ed. Terrell Carver. Cambridge: Cambridge University Press.

———. 2007. *Economic and Philosophic Manuscripts of 1844,* trans. Martin Milligan. Mineola: Dover Publications.

———. 2009. *A Contribution to the Critique of Political Economy,* trans. S. Ryazanskaya. (Moscow: Progress Publishers, 1989), *Marxists Internet Archive,* https://www.marxists.org/archive/marx/works/1859/critique-pol-economy/.

Marx, Karl, and Friedrich Engels. 1963. *Werke,* Vol. 29. Berlin: Dietz Verlag.

———. 1971. *Werke,* Vol. 13. Berlin: Dietz Verlag.

Mason, Paul. 2015. *Postcapitalism: A Guide to Our Future.* London: Penguin Random House.

McNally, David. 2011. *Monsters of the Market: Zombies, Vampires and Global Capitalism.* Leiden: Brill.

Mirowski, Philip. 1988. *Against Mechanism: Protecting Economics from Science.* Lanham: Rowman & Littlefield Publishers.

———. 1989. *More Heat than Light: Economics as Social Physics, Physics as Nature's Economics.* Cambridge: Cambridge University Press.

———. 1993. "The Goalkeeper's Anxiety at the Penalty Kick." In *Non-Natural Social Science: Reflecting on the Enterprise of More Heat than Light,* ed. Neil de Marchi, 305–49. Durham: Duke University Press.

Moseley, Fred, ed. 1993. *Marx's Method in* Capital. Atlantic Highlands: Humanities Press.

———. 1997. "Money Has No Price." Paper presentation, 25th Encontro Nacional de Economia of ANPEC, December 11, 1997, Recife, Brazil, https://www.mtholyoke.edu/~fmoseley/working%20papers/BLAUG.pdf.

————, ed. 2005. *Marx's Theory of Money: Modern Appraisals.* New York: Palgrave Macmillan.

Moseley, Fred and Martha Campbell, eds. 1997. *New Investigations of Marx's Method.* Atlantic Highlands: Humanities Press.

Murray, Patrick. 1993. "The Necessity of Money." In *Marx's Method in* Capital, ed. Fred Moseley, 37–61. Atlantic Highlands: Humanities Press.

————. 1997. "Redoubled Empiricism: The Place of Social Form and Formal Causality in Marxian Theory." In *New Investigations in Marx's Method,* eds. Fred Moseley and Martha Campbell, 38–65. Atlantic Highlands: Humanities Press.

————. 1999. "Marx's 'Truly Social' Labour Theory of Value: Part I, Abstract Labour in Marxian Value Theory." *Historical Materialism* 6, no. 1: 27–66; https://doi.org/10.1163/15692060 0100414551.

————. 2000. "Marx's 'Truly Social' Labour Theory of Value: Part II, How Is Labour that is Under the Sway of Capital *Actually* Abstract?" *Historical Materialism* 7, no. 1: 99–136; https://doi.org/10.1163/15692060100414650.

————. 2005. "Money as Displaced Social Form: Why Value Cannot be Independent of Price." In *Marx's Theory of Money: Modern Appraisals,* ed. Fred Mosely, 50–64. New York: Palgrave Macmillan.

"Myth." *New Oxford American Dictionary.* 3rd ed. Edited by Angus Stevenson and Christine A. Lindberg. Oxford: Oxford University Press, 2015.

Nelson, Julie A. 2006. *Economics for Humans.* Chicago: University of Chicago Press.

Nietzsche, Friedrich. 1967. *On the Genealogy of Morals,* trans. Walter Kaufmann. New York: Vintage Books.

Oakeshott, Michael. 1962. *Rationalism in Politics and Other Essays.* New York: Basic Books Publishing.

Pettifor, Ann. 2014. *Just Money: How Society Can Break the Despotic Power of Finance.* Margate: Commonwealth Publishing.

Petty, William. 1662. *A Treatise of Taxes and Contributions.* London: Printed for N. Brooke.

Piketty, Thomas. 2014. *Capital in the Twenty-First Century,* trans. Arthur Goldhammer. Cambridge: Harvard University Press.

Postone, Moishe. 1993. *Time, Labor, and Social Domination: A Reinterpretation of Marx's Critical Theory.* Cambridge: Cambridge University Press.

Quesnay, François. 1924. *Tableau économique* (1759). In *Early Economic Thought,* ed. Arthur Eli Monroe, 336–48. Cambridge: Harvard University Press; https://www.marxists.org/reference/subject/economics/quesnay/1759/tableau.htm.

Rebrovick, Arthur J. 2016. "Routine Maintenance: Forming, Reforming, and Transforming Social Formations." PhD diss., Johns Hopkins University.

Reckard, E. Scott. 2013a. "Wells Fargo Accuses Workers of Opening Fake Accounts to Meet Goals." *Los Angeles Times,* October 3, http://articles.latimes.com/2013/oct/03/business/la-fi-1004-wells-fargo-firings-20131004.

———. 2013b. "Wells Fargo's Pressure-Cooker Sales Culture Comes at a Cost." *Los Angeles Times,* December 21, http://www.latimes.com/business/la-fi-wells-fargo-sale-pressure-20131222-story.html.

Reichelt, Helmut. 1995. "Why did Marx Conceal His Dialectical Method?" In *Open Marxism,* Vol. 3, eds. Werner Bonefeld, Richard Gunn, John Holloway and Kosmas Psychopedis, 40–83. London: Pluto Press.

Reuten, Geert. 2000. "The Interconnection of Systematic Dialectics and Historical Materialism." *Historical Materialism* 7, no. 1: 137–65; https://doi.org/10.1163/156920600100414669.

Ricardo, David. 2001. *Principles of Political Economy and Taxation.* Kitchener: Batoche Books.

Roberts, William Clare. 2017. *Marx's Inferno: The Political Theory of* Capital. Princeton: Princeton University Press.

Rorty, Richard. 1982. *Consequences of Pragmatism.* Minneapolis: University of Minnesota Press.

Rosdolsky, Roman. 1977. *The Making of Marx's Capital*. London: Pluto Press.

Rubin, Isaac Illich. 1979. *A History of Economic Thought,* trans. Don Filtzer. London: Ink Links.

———. 2008. *Essays on Marx's Theory of Value*. Detroit: Black & Red, 1972. https://www.marxists.org/archive/rubin/value/index.htm.

Samuelson, Paul A. and William D. Nordhaus. 2010. *Economics*. 19th edn. New York: McGraw-Hill.

Schoenberger, Erica. 2008. "The Origins of the Market Economy: State Power, Territorial Control, and Modes of War Fighting." *Comparative Studies in Society and History* 50, no. 3: 663–91; https://doi.org/10.1017/S0010417508000297.

Schulz, Guido. 2012. "Marx's Distinction Between the Fetish Character of the Commodity and Fetishism." *Studies in Social and Political Thought* 20: 25–45.

Sedgwick, Eve Kosofsky. 1990. *Epistemology of The Closet*. Berkeley: University of California Press.

Smith, Adam. 1869. *Essays of Adam Smith*. London: Murray.

———. 1999. *The Wealth of Nations, Books I–III*. London: Penguin Books.

Sraffa, Piero. 1951. Introduction to *The Works and Correspondence of David Ricardo,* Vol. 1, eds. Piero Sraffa and Maurice H. Dobb, xiii–lxii. Cambridge: Cambridge University Press.

———. 1960. *Production of Commodities by Means of Commodities: Prelude to a Critique of Economic Theory*. Cambridge: Cambridge University Press.

Steuart, James. 1767. *An Inquiry into the Principles of Political Economy*. Vol. 1. London: Millar & Cadell.

Stout, Lynn. 2012. *The Shareholder Value Myth: How Putting Shareholders First Harms Investors, Corporations, and the Public*. San Francisco: Berrett-Koehler Publishers.

"Supply and Demand." 2018. *Wikipedia,* https://en.wikipedia.org/wiki/Supply_and_demand#History.

Taylor, Charles. 1985. *Human Agency and Language: Philosophical Papers 1*. Cambridge: Cambridge University Press.

"Value." *Oxford English Dictionary,* http://www.oed.com.

Vatter, Miguel. 2014. *The Republic of the Living: Biopolitics and the Critique of Civil Society.* New York: Fordham University Press.

Veblen, Thorstein. 1900. "The Preconceptions of Economic Science." *The Quarterly Journal of Economics* 14, no. 2: 240–69; https://doi.org/10.2307/1883770.

Vernon, Pete. 2016. "Q&A: Former LA *Times* Reporter on Story that Led to $185 Million Wells Fargo Fine." *Columbia Journalism Review,* September 12, https://www.cjr.org/q_and_a/wells_fargo_la_times_accounts.php.

Wood, Ellen Meiksins. 2016. *The Origin of Capitalism: A Longer View.* London: Verso.

Wells Fargo. 2016. "The Vision and Values of Wells Fargo." *Wells Fargo Media,* https://web.archive.org/web/20161114221820/https://www.wellsfargo.com/about/corporate/vision-and-values/index.

Wittgenstein, Ludwig. 2009. *Philosophical Investigations,* trans. G.E.M. Anscombe, P.M.S. Hacker, and Joachim Schulte. Chichester: Wiley Blackwell.

Wolff, Robert Paul. 1981. "A Critique and Reinterpretation of Marx's Labor Theory of Value." *Philosophy and Public Affairs* 10, no. 2: 89–120; http://www.jstor.org/stable/2264974.

Acknowledgments_

Every book comes into existence through an array and alliance of forces that far exceed the work of the so-called author, but for me that fact has never been more true than in the case of this work. Taken in its broadest terms, my project here is to make some sense out of the "nature" of value within a social order structured by the logic of capital. However, the question of value has always been at the heart of writings on capitalism: from the corpus of classical political economy, to Marx and Marxism, right through — at least in sublimated fashion in the price form — to the neoclassical paradigm of modern Economics. Since I did not wish to pretend to reinvent the wheel, I have tried to base my own work on what I see as the very best writings on value across that very wide swath of historical texts. My debts here are clearly marked in the book, but they run so deep that I feel the urge to delineate them in this space as well: to Marx's mid-nineteenth-century readings of the classical political economists, to Philip Mirowski's late nineteenth- and early twentieth-century history of economic thought, and to the value-form theorists' late twentieth- and early twenty-first-century work. I especially underscore this last acknowledgement, since it has been truly shocking to me to see how many authors have written on Marx and value in the past two decades without mentioning the names of any of the value-form theorists.

Mark Devenney almost singlehandedly carved out the intellectual space for the production of this book. Large portions of it were written and first publicly presented while I was a Leverhulme Visiting Professor at the University of Brighton in spring and then winter of 2016. I got a fancy title, the financial support to be in Brighton and travel around the UK and continental Europe, and the opportunity to present work in progress to a variety of wonderful academic and public audiences; Mark got to fill out a lot of complicated grant application forms and deal with large amounts of red tape. I am astonished by the support and generosity that Mark extended to a colleague he had never even met, and I will forever be grateful to him. However, I say *almost* singlehandedly, because another great benefit of my time in Brighton was the chance to be surrounded by an intellectually diverse and vibrant community of scholars — the same group that surrounds Mark every day. At Brighton, I thank: Bob Brecher, Thomas Bunyard, Lars Cornelissen, Tim Huzar, Andy Knott, Anthony Leaker, Toby Lovat, Michael Neu, German Primera, Rebecca Searle, Ian Sinclair, and Clare Woodford. I also thank all the participants in the seminars and reading groups I ran while in Brighton, and all the audience members who attended my Leverhulme Lectures and Political Studies Association presentations. Here I also wish to acknowledge formally the Leverhulme Trust, for the grant that supported my Visiting Leverhulme Professorship in Brighton.

While stationed in Brighton I piled up debts to numerous others at nearby institutions. At Queen Mary University of London, I thank Jean-Francois Drolet, Kim Hutchings, Lasse Thomassen, and a number of great audience questioners whose names I never caught. At the University of Vienna, I think Oliver Marchart, Anna-Teresa Steffner, and faculty members of the Department of Political Science. At the University of Newcastle, I thank Jemima Repo, Simon Philpott, and Matt Davies. At the London School of Economics workshop, I thank George Lawson, Tarak Barkawi, Daniel Levine, Jahn Beate, Helen Kinsella, David Blaney, and Patricia Owens. At the University of East Anglia, I thank Alan Finlayson, Michael Frazer, and Sophia Hatz-isavvidou.

Back on the other side of the Atlantic, I am particularly grateful to seminar participants in the Johns Hopkins Political and Moral Thought Seminar, November 2016, for a lively and stimulating discussion of a core piece of the manuscript at just the right moment in its development. Among a larger group, let me specifically record my gratitude to: John Marshall, Jane Bennett, Angus Bergin, PJ Brendese, Bill Connolly, Ali Khan, Jon Masin-Peters, Sebastian Mazzuca, Ken Moss, Zachary Reyna, and Erica Schoenberger. One of the final appraisals of the book was given by the students in my Spring 2017 graduate seminar. I note my deep appreciation for the close readings and critical engagements by the entire group; in particular, I thank Meghaa Ballakrishnen for catching some errors that everyone else (including myself) had missed. At Hopkins I also rely (more than they know) on the collegiality and support of a number of colleagues who always have my back: Bentley Allan, Jennifer Culbert, Lester Spence, and Emily Zackin.

Lisa Disch, Tripp Rebrovick, and Terrell Carver all gave detailed feedback on key portions of the book at a pivotal time in its development. Lisa and Tripp helped me choose a heading, and Terrell gave me the key push I needed to go there. Patrick Giamario read all or parts of the book on at least three different occasions and at the end of the project his copy-editing and work on the citational apparatus proved invaluable. Getting to write a book with the aid and support of one's own PhD students—brilliant and hardworking thinkers and writers who know your own thought and language inside and out—is a privilege beyond measure. I honestly wonder if it should count as cheating, but since it remains accepted practice, I am proud to thank Pat directly here. Some of Pat's RA work was funded by the Department of Political Science at Johns Hopkins; I thank the Department Chair, Adam Sheingate, for that and much other help and support.

Portions of chapter 2 and a few reworked passages from chapter 3 were previously published in *Political Power and So-*

cial Theory, vol 32, pp. 63–98, 2017. I thank the editor of *PPST,* Julian Go, and Emerald Publishing for the right to reuse that material here.

This book, in this particular shape and form, would certainly not have come into existence without the vision and support of Eileen Joy, whose enthusiasm for the project proved an inspiration to me all along the way. I am deeply grateful to Eileen for her efforts as editor on this book, but more than that, I also want to acknowledge here her courageous work with the project that is punctum books. Sincere thanks also go to Eileen's co-director, Vincent W.J. van Gerven Oei, for his outstanding and professional work on the interior design, typesetting, and layout of the book. Every author knows that cover designs always prove to be sources of anxiety and often of disappointment, but I could not be more thrilled with the result here, and therefore do not have the words to express my gratitude to publishing lab student Madison Mead for her outstanding efforts. Last but certainly not least, I thank the other publishing lab students who worked on the book, especially at the copyediting stage: Annette Ding and Noah Feiwell.

In addition to Brighton and Baltimore, portions of this book were written in our new-found and newly made home further west, Portland, where I am grateful and lucky to have family, friends, and community. For providing that essential—yet impalpable, intangible and often ephemeral—space to flourish, I thank: Tamara Metz, Jackie Chambers, Tim Chambers, Marsha Manning, Pete Aller, Alan Smith, Christie Snyder, Owen Snyder-Smith, Joel Bettridge, Liz Ceppi, Paul Mariz, Laurie Frankel, Andrew Valls, and Jessica Burness. Home is where people come to visit you, and I am grateful to our guests in Portland who helped to make the place special for us: Stephanie Brown, Liz Doris, Katherine Hammer, Jason Hammer, Stephanie Hershinow, Travis Doris, David Hershinow, Alex Livingston, Merike Andre-Barrett, Eric Appleton, Alex Cuervo, Julian Brown, and Jane Elliott. I would be deeply remiss if I failed to thank baristas far and wide, in particular those at Ristretto, Case Study, and Heart in PDX, and those at Bond Street and Pharmacie in Brighton.

The roots for this book can be traced back to early 2010 when I read Marx's *Capital* closely and carefully for the first time. In the process, I repeatedly subjected Rebecca Brown to loud out-bursts of laughter (it's a very funny book). She tolerated not only those disruptions of her own work, but also the numerous times over the years when I would interrupt a normal conversation (or the viewing of a film or TV show) in order to launch a discourse that subjected just about any imaginable event or phenomenon in the world to a value-form analysis. In allowing me to teach her the logic of capital, she gave me the opportunity to learn it myself (i.e., she taught me). Later on she joined me in reading Marx—thereby coming to agree with me about its humor—and in so doing she inflected and shaped a number of elements of my own reading as presented in this book. As with everything else I write or make or achieve, Rebecca is the condition of (im)possibility for this work.

I have previously written about the power of a pedagogy based upon a radical principle of equality. This principle is not a normative rule or an empirical truth, but an *assumption* made by only the best teachers when they refuse the idea, so central to so much traditional pedagogy, that their intelligence is su-perior to that of their students — when they make the opposite assumption, that the student can understand perfectly well be-cause of the equality of intelligence. Hence what makes a great teacher is the ability, the willingness, and the courage *to grant students the gift* of the assumption of equality. I have been deeply fortunate to have a number of fantastic teachers over the years who extended that gift to me: Betty Klein, Sister Joel Christoph, Roberta Noland, Lee McDonald, and Lisa Disch. I dedicate this book to them.

Printed in Great Britain
by Amazon

40715704R00096